201 *Cross-Stitch* Christmas Designs™

by Kooler Design Studio

Editorial: Bobbie Matela, Carol Wilson Mansfield, April McArthur, Christina Wilson, Kathy Wesley, Shirley Patrick
Production: Joanne Gonzalez
Photography: Scott Campbell, Andy Burnfield, Martha Coquat, Crystal Key

Pictured models were stitched by Christina Bowen, Jill Brooks, Debra Brown, Barbara Chancy, Chris Cochran, Betty Curran, Lorraine Giera, Ellen Harnden, Pat Hyland, Sandi Kardack, Sandy Kennebeck, Bobbie Matela, Wendy Mathson, April McArthur, Helen McClaine, Sue McVae, Maxine Meadows, Deborah Michael, Pam Mollahan, Mary Alice Patsko, Sue Reagan, Lisa Suycott, Lee Ann Tibbals, Kathy Wesley and Christina Wilson.

Cross-stitch charts by: Kathryn Causee, Lisa DeLasaux, April McArthur, Deborah Michael and Christina Wilson.

Thank you to the following companies who generously supplied products for our models:
Coats & Clark, Anchor floss
Charles Craft, Fabric and ready-made product
Crafter's Pride, Ready-made product
Michell Marketing, Assorted hangers
Zweigart, Fabric

1455 Linda Vista Drive
San Marcos, CA 92069
www.ASNpub.com
© 2003 by Kooler Design Studio Inc.

The full line of ASN products is carried by Annie's Attic catalog.
TOLL FREE ORDER LINE or to request a free catalog (800) 582-6643
Customer Service (800) 282-6643, **Fax** (800) 882-6643
Visit www.AnniesAttic.com

We have made every effort to ensure the accuracy and completeness of these instructions. We cannot, however, be responsible for human error, typographical mistakes or variations in individual work. Reprinting or duplicating the information, photographs or graphics in this publication by any means, including copy machine, computer scanning, digital photography, e-mail, personal Web site and fax, is illegal. Failure to abide by federal copyright laws may result in litigation and fines.

ISBN: 1-59012-043-4   Library of Congress: 2003103992   All rights reserved.   Printed in USA   1 2 3 4 5 6 7 8 9

Introduction

Christmas is a joyous season of gift giving and spending time with loved ones. This wonderful assortment of 201 designs will provide you with just the right projects to stitch as gifts or to decorate your home.

Choose from nostalgic designs inspired by days gone by, modern designs with a techno edge and whimsical delights to put a twinkle in any Santa's eye.

We thank Kooler Design Studio for sharing their design talents so we can all create beautiful stitchery and spread the spirit of giving each holiday season.

From the Twelve Days of Christmas Santa Sampler beginning on page 4

From the Twelve Days of Christmas Old Fashioned Sampler beginning on page 116

From the Twelve Days of Christmas Baby Sampler beginning on page 93

From the Sporty Santa Sampler beginning on page 37

General Directions 125–126
Finishing Information 127
Index of Charts by Subject 128

1–12 Twelve Days of Christmas Santa Sampler

Design size: 211 wide x 332 high

	Anchor	DMC		Anchor	DMC
	2	blanc	△	928	3761
□	366	951	⌃	1032	3752
♡	24	963	⊠	1033	932
∪	1024	3328	⌇	1060	3811
■	46	666	~	128	775
■	43	814	□	129	809
~	778	3774	O	1038	519
△	868	758	▶	136	799
O	330	947	☆	1039	518
✕	326	720	■	132	797
□	300	745	⬠	85	3609
+	301	744	□	96	3608
◇	302	743	▽	342	211
□	305	726	⌇	97	554
✕	311	677	□	98	553
★	306	783	⊕	109	209
◉	891	676	⊠	881	945
△	253	472	□	883	3772
⊠	204	563	~	347	3064
□	240	966	O	368	437
⌃	225	703	+	914	407
+	226	701	♡	349	301
◇	238	702	◆	355	975
♡	241	704	◩	369	435
✳	210	562	⌃	884	356
◤	246	986	■	1007	3859
⊠	211	561	⌃	1047	402
■	245	987	▣	1048	3776
~	956	613	□	234	762
+	945	834	◇	235	414
□	260	3364	■	399	318
◇	261	989	■	403	310

French Knots:
979/312–lettering
403/310–birds' eyes

Backstitch:
46/666—pear string, 10th day box spots, 11th day sock plaid
212/561—leaves
979/312—lettering, fifth day white gem
884/356—skin, first day pear and tree trunk, second day nest and buckle, third day chick, fifth day rings (except gems), sixth day buckle, beaks and straw, seventh day beak, ninth day female hair and Santa buckle, 12th day drumsticks
211/562–fourth day shirt stripes
978/322–seventh day water
357/300–eighth day hat, buckle, bucket
244/987–ninth day sleeve stripes, comb teeth
245/986–11th day string, dog's hat plaid, remaining sock plaid
1007/3772–10th day boots, buckles, bells (except slits)
400/317—remaining outlines
403/310—all eyes, belts and boots (except for 11th day boots), fourth day birds, 10th day bell slits and straps, 11th day dog and shoes, 12th day hats and drum straps

A Partridge in a Pear Tree

Four Calling Birds

Five

Continue stitching from chart on page 8

Continue stitching from chart on page 7

6 • 201 Cross-Stitch Christmas Designs

For color key see page 5

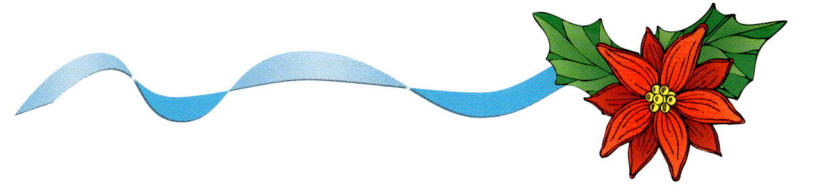

Two Turtle Doves

Three French Hens

Continue stitching from chart on page 9

201 Cross-Stitch Christmas Designs • 7

Continue stitching from chart on page 6

Golden Rings

Seven Swans a-Swimming

Continue stitching from chart on page 10

For color key see page 5

Continue stitching from chart on page 7

Six Geese-a-Laying

Continue stitching from chart on page 11

201 Cross-Stitch Christmas Designs • 9

Continue stitching from chart on page 8

Eight Maids

Ten Lords a-Leaping

Continue stitching from chart on page 11

Eleve

10 • 201 Cross-Stitch Christmas Designs

For color key see page 5

Continue stitching from chart on page 9

-a-Milking   Nine Ladies Dancing

n Pipers Piping   Twelve Drummers Drumming

201 Cross-Stitch Christmas Designs • 11

13

Design size: 24 wide x 44 high

Anchor	DMC
2	blanc
50	3716
47	321
44	815
1012	754
314	741
326	720
302	743
226	703
142	798
231	453
403	310

Backstitch:
47/47—mouth
44/815—hat (except band and brim), suit (except cuffs and sides of blue trim), buttons
923/699—tree (except trunk), sash
351/400—hat band, cuffs, tree ornament, tree trunk
403/310—remaining outlines

14

Design size: 25 wide x 44 high

Anchor	DMC
2	blanc
50	3716
47	321
44	815
1012	754
314	741
326	720
302	743
226	703
142	798
231	453

Backstitch:
47/321—mouth
44/815—suit
923/699—tree
351/400—hat
403/310—remaining outlines

15

Design size: 25 wide x 42 high

Anchor	DMC
2	blanc
50	3716
1012	754
314	741
326	720
302	743
226	703
229	910
1070	993
110	208
231	453
403	310

Backstitch:
47/321—mouth
923/699–green hat edges, bottom green suit edges
351/400—star, staff, remaining hat, cuffs, gold coat trim
403/310—remaining edges

16

Design size: 31 wide x 29 high

Anchor	DMC
300	745
46	666
47	321
323	722
295	726
311	676
1002	977
225	703

Backstitch:
330/947—flame
212/561—leaves
1049/301—holder
401/317—wick, candle

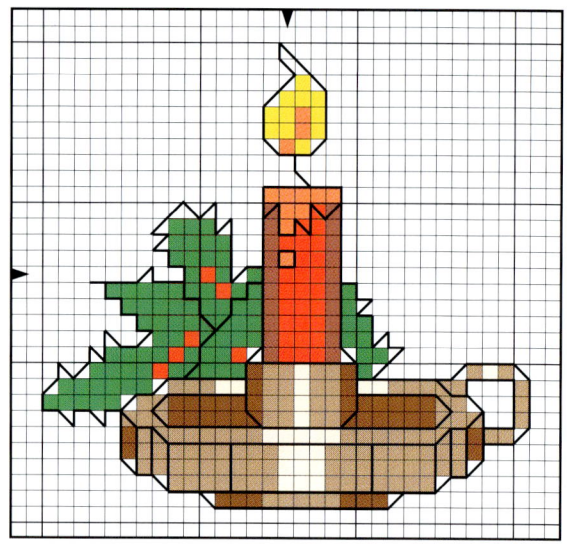

17

Design size: 22 wide x 36 high

Anchor	DMC
2	blanc
9046	666
1005	816
314	741
324	721
300	745
302	743
226	703
229	910
923	699
231	453
403	310

Backstitch:
1005/816—berry
326/720—flame, holder
923/699—leaves
403/310—candle

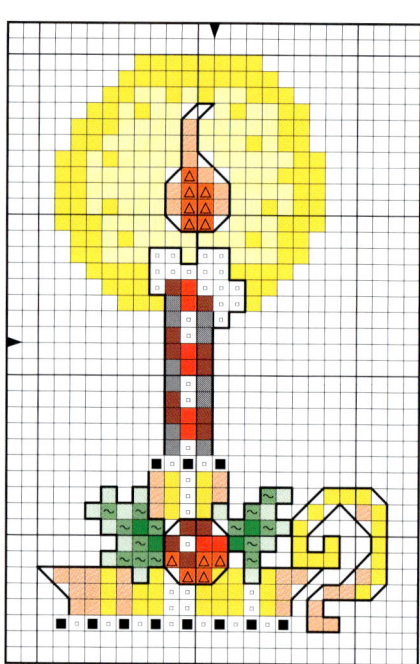

14 • 201 Cross-Stitch Christmas Designs

18

Design size: 20 wide x 16 high

Anchor	DMC
☐ 361	738
895	223
~ 9	352
11	351
363	436
369	435

Backstitch:
896/3721—bow
370/434—bone

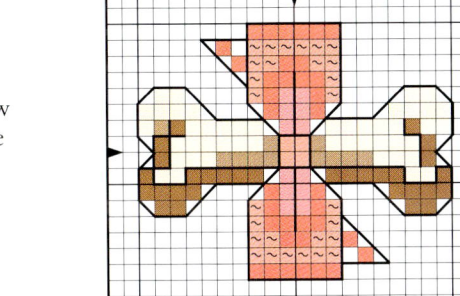

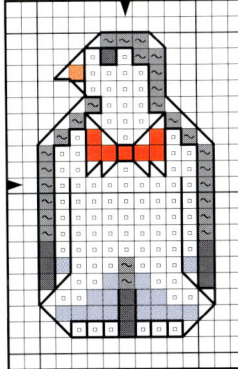

19

Design size: 11 wide x 19 high

Anchor	DMC
∘ 2	blanc
1098	3801
323	722
1032	3752
~ 399	318
235	414

Backstitch:
47/321—bow
324/721—beak
401/413—remaining penguin

201 Cross-Stitch Christmas Designs • 15

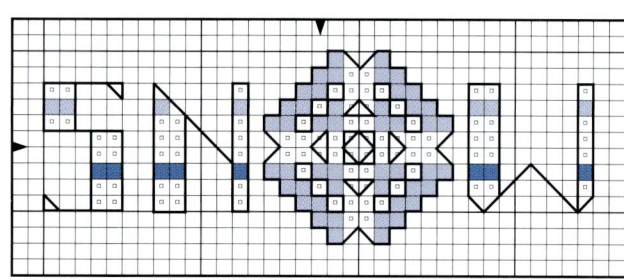

20

Design size: 35 wide x 12 high

Anchor	DMC
2	blanc
128	775
160	827

Backstitch:
161/813—snowflake
979/312—letters

21

Design size: 33 wide x 17 high

Anchor	DMC
2	blanc
46	666
47	321
225	703
210	562

Backstitch:
1005/816—letters, bow
217/561—wreath

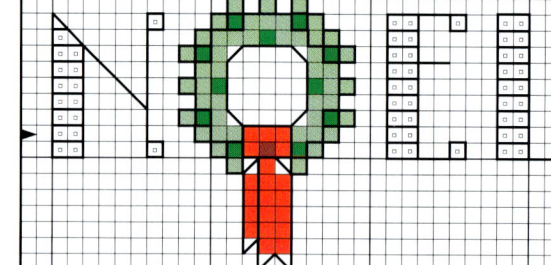

22

Design size: 40 wide x 19 high

Anchor	DMC
2	blanc
8	353
11	351
206	564
342	211
96	3609
98	553

Backstitch:
13/347—border
877/501—letters
100/552—ornament

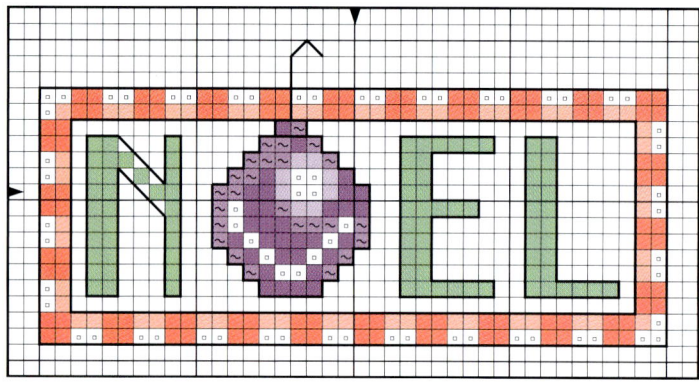

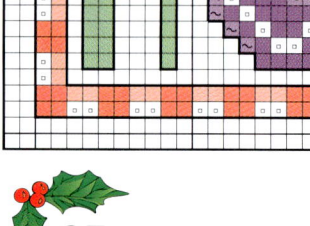

23

Design size: 39 wide x 16 high

Anchor	DMC
2	blanc
36	3326
38	961
42	326
43	814
203	564

Backstitch:
43/814—ornament
217/561—lettering

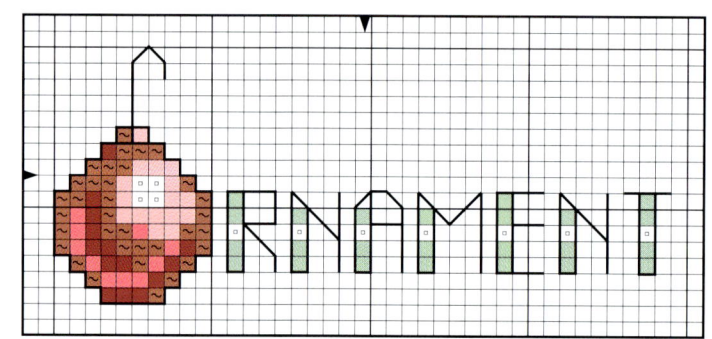

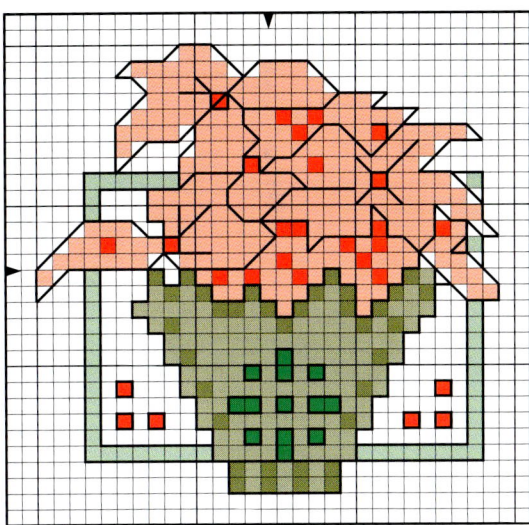

24

Design size: 29 wide x 28 high

Anchor	DMC
13	347
11	351
253	472
225	703
206	564
210	562

Backstitch:
22/814—plant, dots
212/561—frame, pot

25

Design size: 25 wide x 36 high

Anchor	DMC
33	3706
46	666
203	564
160	827

Backstitch (2 strands):
19/304—chimney, berries
211/562—leaves, trees
161/813—snow, border, roof
349/301—remaining house
235/414—smoke

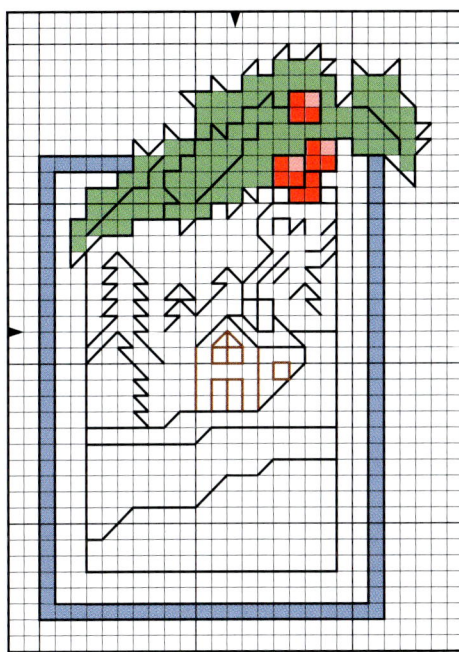

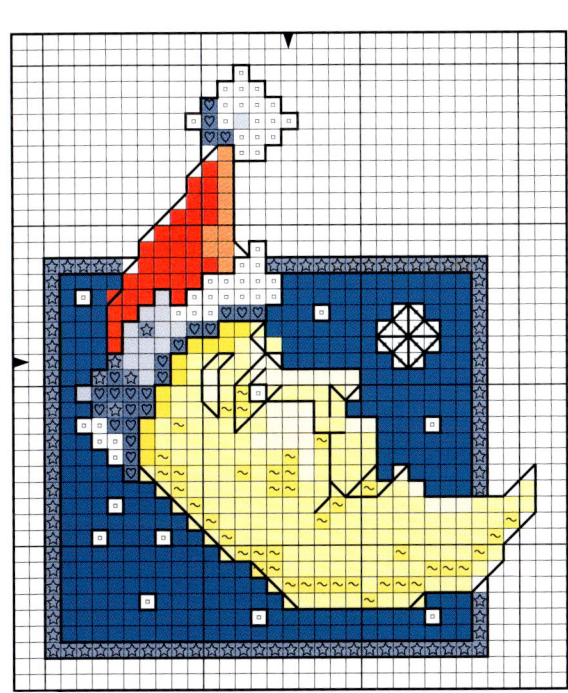

26

Design size: 31 wide x 37 high

Anchor	DMC
2	blanc
386	3823
46	666
329	3340
301	744
302	743
1002	977
128	775
160	827
920	932
979	312

Eyelet (star): 305/743
Backstitch: 149/322

27

Design size: 54 wide x 43 high

Anchor	DMC
2	blanc
24	963
778	3774
868	758
9	352
11	351
311	676
313	742
367	738
1045	436
206	564
208	563
217	561
128	775
129	809
176	793
400	317

French Knots: 401/413

Straight Stitch
(scarf fringe):
13/347—red scarf
176/793—blue scarf

Backstitch:
1002/977—hair curl
176/793—hat fur trims, snow, blue mug, mittens
401/413—remaining outlines

28

Design size: 45 wide x 44 high

Anchor	DMC
2	blanc
26	894
778	3774
868	758
11	351
301	744
302	743
206	564
208	563
210	562
186	959
128	775
176	793
882	950
883	3064
235	414

French Knots: 401/310

Straight Stitch
(scarf fringe): 188/3812

Backstitch:
13/347—bell zigzags
217/561—bell zigzags
188/3812—bell string
136/799—hat, snow
401/310—remaining outlines

29

Design size: 94 wide x 36 high

Anchor	DMC
2	blanc
46	666
259	772
206	564
208	563
1092	959

French Knots:

305/743 (yellow)—second "R" in "Merry," "C"
46/666—second "R" in "Merry," "C"
110/798—second "R" in "Merry," "C"

Eyelets:

142/798—first "R" in "Merry," both "S's"
110/208—first "R" in "Merry," both "S's"

Backstitch:

46/666— "M," Stripes in the "E" and "Y" in "Merry";
Stripes in the "H," "R," "I," "M," "A" in "Christmas"
210/562— Stripes in the "M," "E," "Y" in "Merry";
Stripes in the "I," "T" in "Christmas"
1074/992— second "R" in "Merry," ; "C," "H" in "Christmas"
142/798— both "R's" in "Merry," ; "C," both "S's" in "Christmas"

20 • *201 Cross-Stitch Christmas Designs*

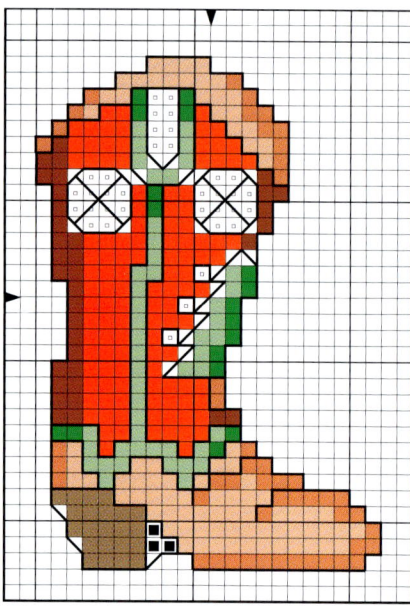

30

Design size: 22 wide x 32 high

Anchor	DMC
2	blanc
47	321
44	915
226	703
229	910
1047	402
1048	3776
903	640
403	310

Backstitch: 403/310

31

Design size: 36 wide x 45 high

Anchor	DMC
2	blanc
13	347
778	3774
868	758
10	351
203	564
160	827
1032	3752
234	762
399	318
235	414

French Knots: 400/317

Backstitch:
235/414—helmet glass, air lines, rocket smoke
400/317—remaining outlines

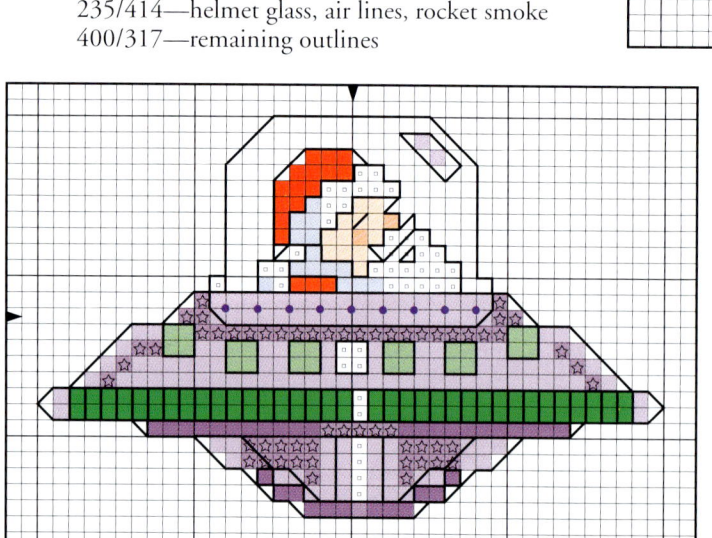

32

Design size: 40 wide x 25 high

Anchor	DMC
2	blanc
46	666
778	3774
868	758
206	564
203	954
128	775
342	211
108	210
110	208

French Knots:
111/3837

Backstitch:
109/209—
saucer glass
111/3837—
remaining
outlines

33

Design size: 106 wide x 39 high

Anchor	DMC	Anchor	DMC
2	blanc	259	772
391	303	265	3347
24	963	242	989
1024	3328	210	562
47	321	159	3325
20	815	978	322
778	3774	979	312
300	745	392	642
311	676	398	415
1003	922	403	310

Backstitch:
22/814—banner, banner tracery, hat and suit (except fur trims), red plane edges and plane design
268/937—tree
212/561—lettering, green plane edges
979/312—blue plane edges
1004/920—ribbon
393/640—wing and wheel trims and struts, hand, fur trims, beard
403/310—eyes, front wheel, black plane edges

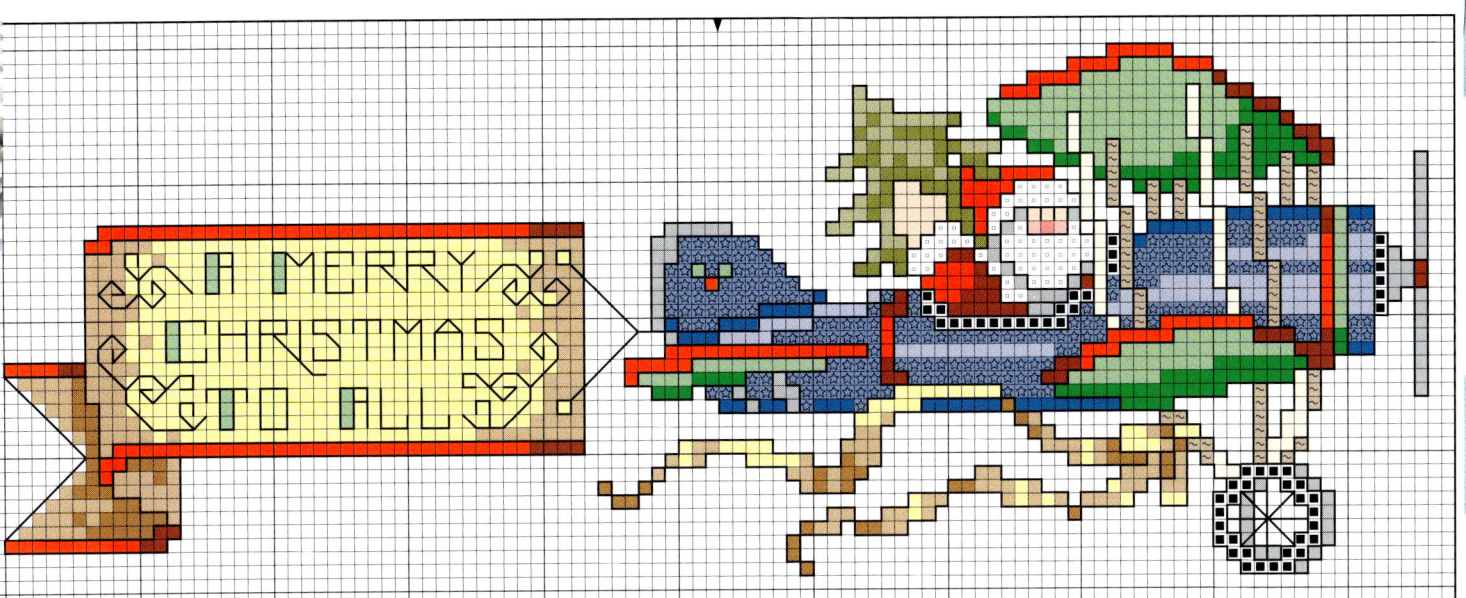

34

Design size: 46 wide x 45 high

Anchor	DMC
2	blanc
1021	761
20	815
778	3774
9	352
11	351
1042	504
875	503
876	502
128	775
129	809
136	799

French Knots: 401/413

Backstitch:
878/501—leaves
401/413—remaining outlines

201 Cross-Stitch Christmas Designs • 23

35

Design size: 45 wide x 37 high

Anchor	DMC
2	blanc
13	347
9	352
11	351
242	989
211	562
9159	3841
1038	519
144	800
161	813

Backstitch:
20/815—hat (except fur trim)
211/562—land
979/312—water, hat trim

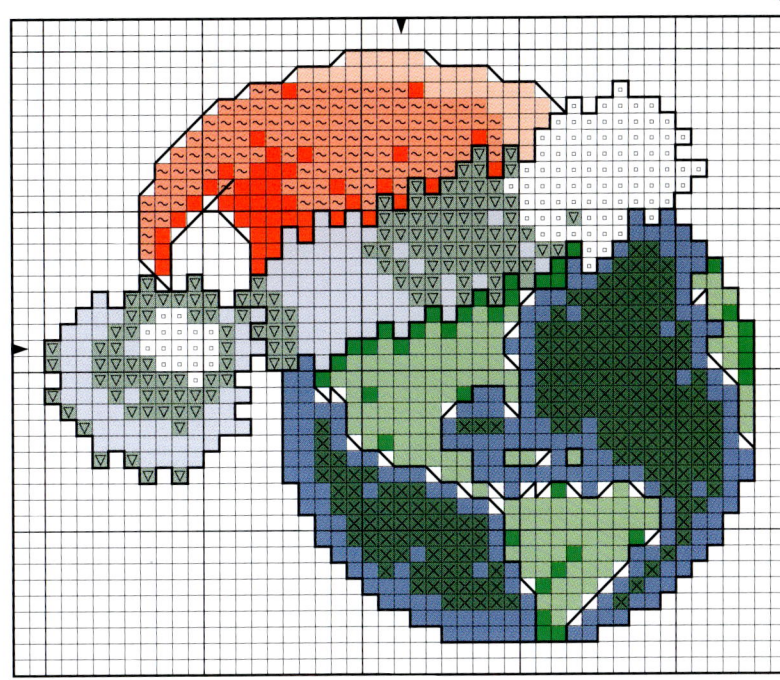

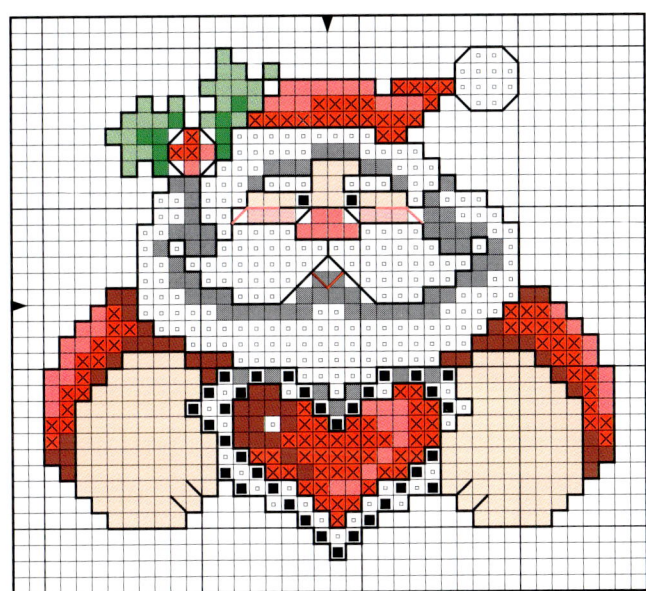

36

Design size: 36 wide x 32 high

Anchor	DMC
2	blanc
50	3716
54	956
9046	666
1005	816
1012	754
226	103
229	910
231	453
403	310

Backstitch:
54/956—cheeks
9046/666—mouth
403/310—remaining outlines

37

Design size: 39 wide x 12 high

Anchor	DMC
2	blanc
46	666
47	321
314	741
329	3340
238	472
347	402
9159	3841

French Knots: 46/666
Eyelet (tree star): 314/741
Backstitch:
46/666—inside "S" and "N"
245/986—letters, tree, house
399/318—chimney smoke

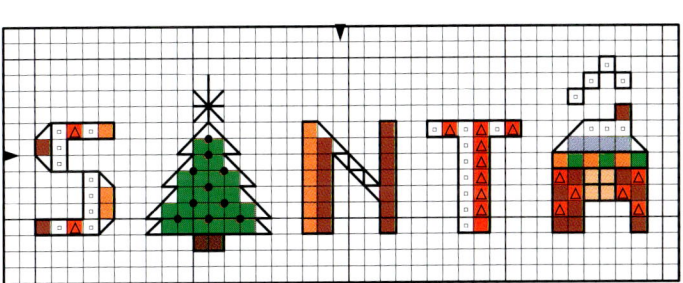

201 Cross-Stitch Christmas Designs • 25

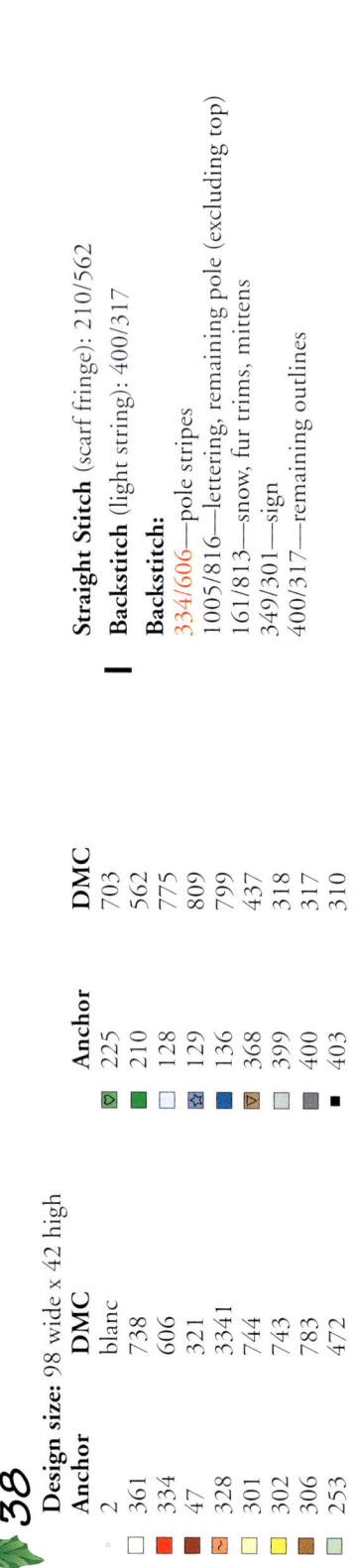

38

Design size: 98 wide x 42 high

Anchor	DMC	
2	blanc	□
361	738	
334	606	■
47	321	
328	3341	◊
301	744	
302	743	
306	783	
253	472	

Anchor	DMC	
225	703	▷
210	562	■
128	775	
129	809	✦
136	799	■
368	437	▷
399	318	
400	317	■
403	310	■

Straight Stitch (scarf fringe): 210/562
Backstitch (light string): 400/317
Backstitch:
334/606—pole stripes
1005/816—lettering, remaining pole (excluding top)
161/813—snow, fur trims, mittens
349/301—sign
400/317—remaining outlines

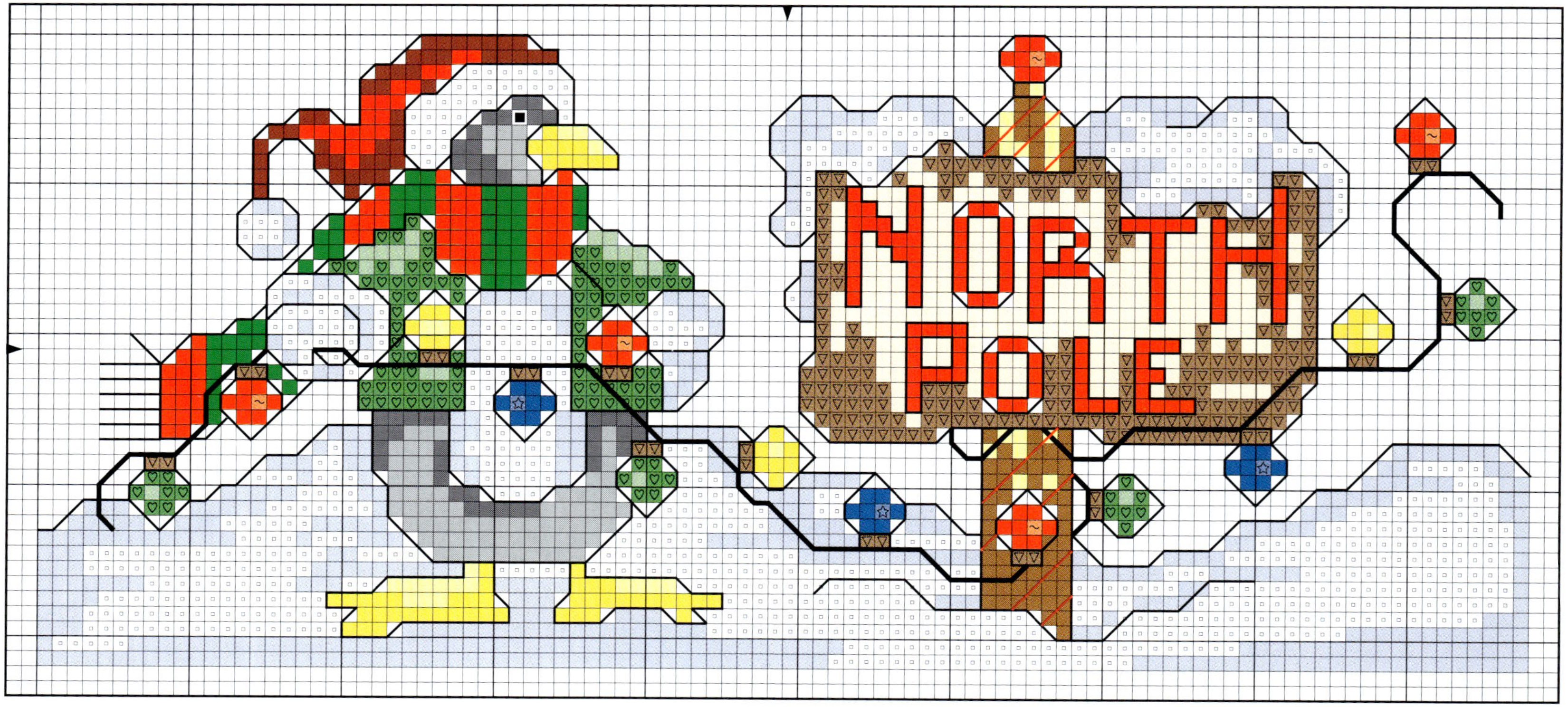

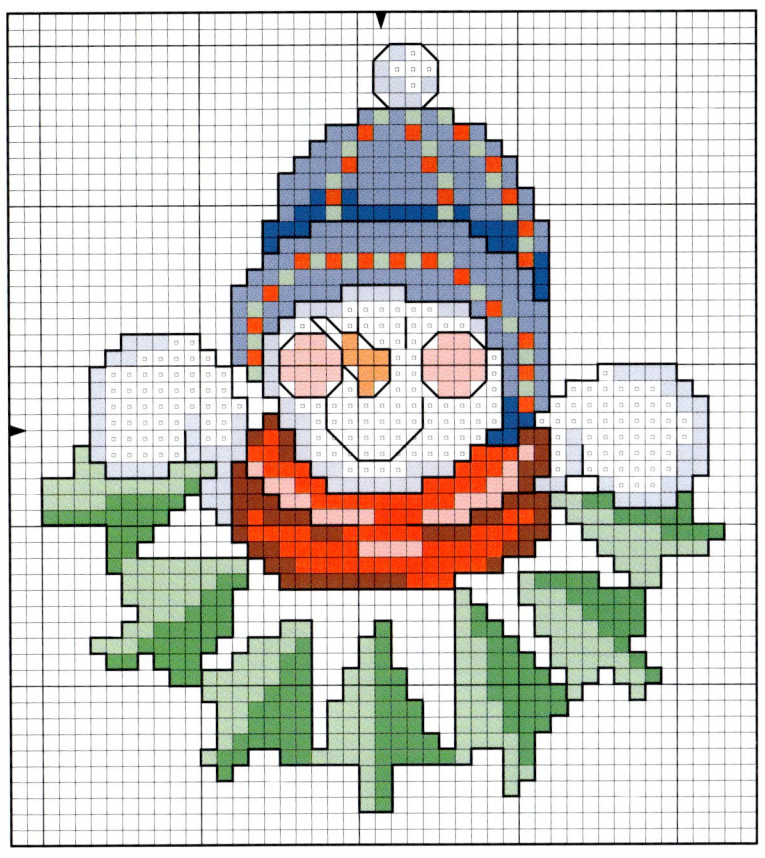

39

Design size: 43 wide x 48 high

Anchor	DMC
2	blanc
40	956
47	321
44	815
324	721
226	703
229	910
128	775
142	798
139	797

Backstitch: 403/310

40

Design size: 30 wide x 46 high
Stitching note: use one strand white to work very small French knots for eye highlights.

Anchor	DMC
2	blanc
54	956
334	606
47	321
44	815
240	966
226	703
1047	402
1048	3776
403	310

Backstitch:
47/321—mouth, nose
226/703—hat, mittens, candy cheeks (except outlines)
351/400—cookies, heart
403/310—cherry stem, eyes, candy cheek outlines

 ## 41

Design size: 49 wide x 30 high

Anchor	DMC
2	blanc
894	223
895	3722
881	945
882	758
300	745
891	676
1042	504
214	368
128	775
234	762
399	318

French Knots: 400/317
Eyelets (stars): 136/799
Backstitch:
1025/347—lamp post bows
136/799—roofs, snow
400/317—remaining outlines

 ## 42

Design size: 21 wide x 20 high

Anchor	DMC
300	745
311	676
1002	977
260	3364
261	989

French Knots: 47/321
Backstitch: 400/317

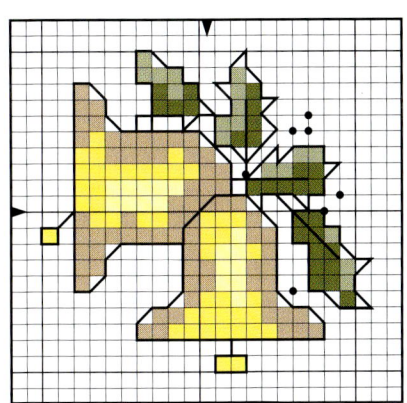

43

Design size: 59 wide x 52 high

Anchor	DMC	Anchor	DMC
2	blanc	206	564
893	738	208	563
74	3354	1042	504
895	223	214	368
13	347	260	3364
11	351	261	989
778	3774	128	775
868	758	108	210
367	738	349	301
347	402	234	762
300	745	399	318
301	744	400	317

French Knots:
13/347—holly berries
877/501—coat buttons
400/317—eyes

Backstitch:
13/347—lamp pole stripes
877/501—scarf stripes, dress stripes
136/799—snow
400/317—remaining outlines

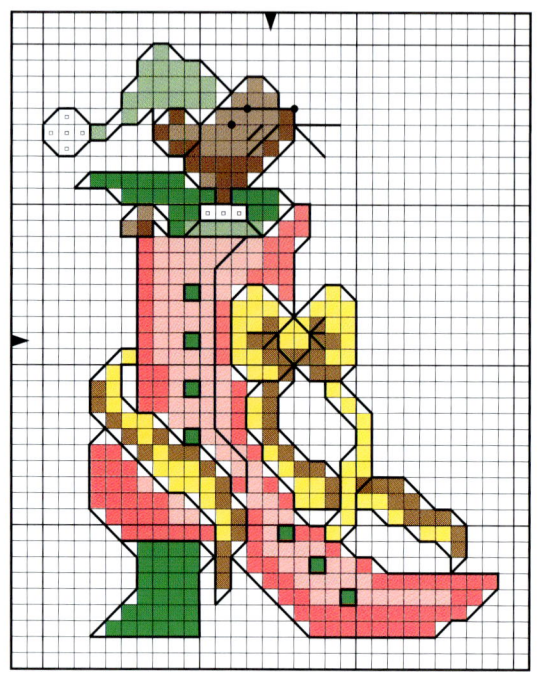

44

Design size: 29 wide x 37 high

Anchor	DMC
2	blanc
894	223
1027	3722
311	676
1002	977
875	503
876	3813
1008	3773
883	3064

French Knots: 401/413
Straight Stitch (whiskers): 401/413
Backstitch: 401/413

45

Design size: 52 wide x 56 high

Anchor	DMC
2	blanc
311	676
334	606
47	321
293	727
1002	977
1048	3776
355	975
214	368
210	562
1031	3753
1033	932
376	3774
379	840
936	632
234	762
399	318
403	310

French Knots (2 strands):
2/blanc—star

Backstitch:
2/blanc (2 strands)—star
1005/816—bird (except beak and foot)
355/975—ribbon border
936/632—stump, cabin siding
401/413—smoke, remaining cabin, snow, trees
403/310—beak, foot

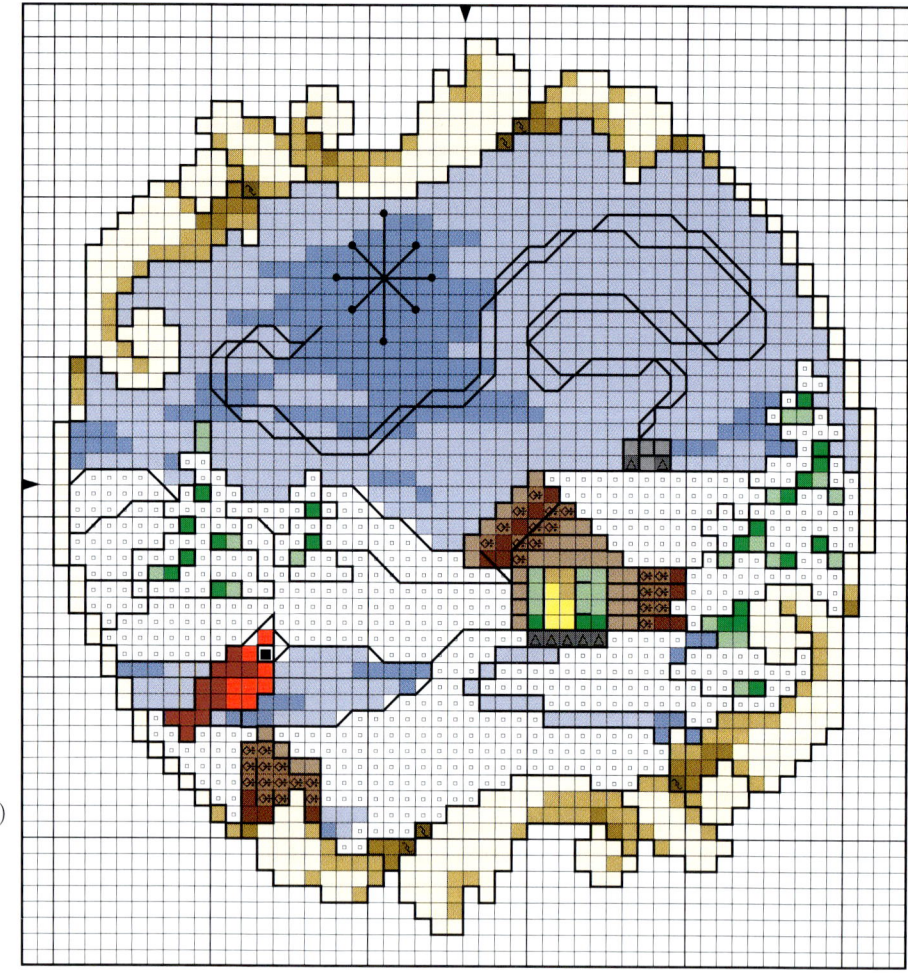

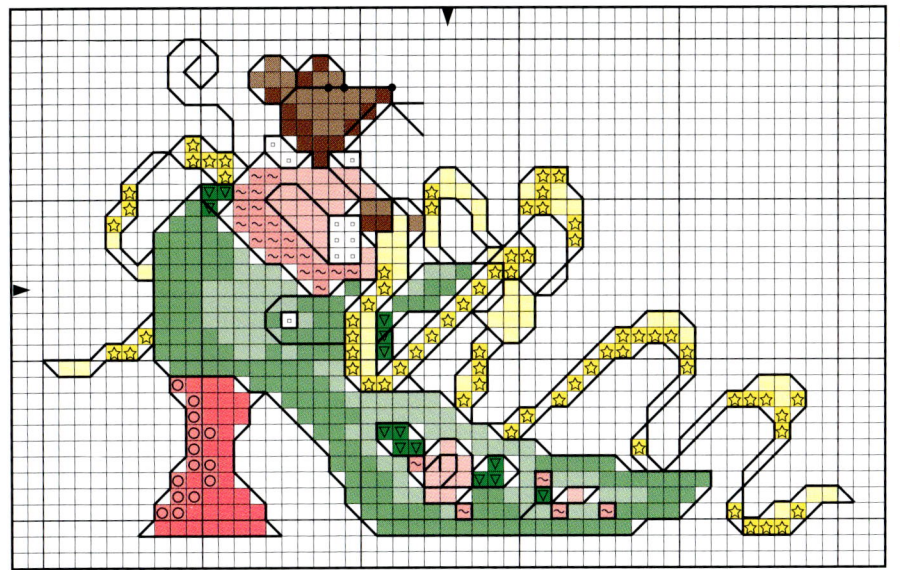

46

Design size: 51 wide x 31 high

Anchor	DMC
2	blanc
75	962
76	961
894	223
1027	3722
300	745
311	676
1042	504
875	503
876	3813
1008	3773
883	3064

French Knots: 401/413
Straigh Stitch (whiskers): 401/413
Backstitch:
1048/3776—ribbon
401/403—remaining outlines

47

Design size: 52 wide x 56 high

Anchor	DMC
2	blanc
311	676
293	727
1002	977
1048	3776
355	975
214	368
210	562
1031	3753
1033	932
376	3774
379	840
397	3042
398	415
399	318
400	317

French Knots:
2/blanc (2 strands)—star
46/666—berries

Backstitch:
2/blanc (2 strands)—star
355/975—ribbon border,
   window leading
379/840—cross, door, branches
401/413—remaining
   church, snow

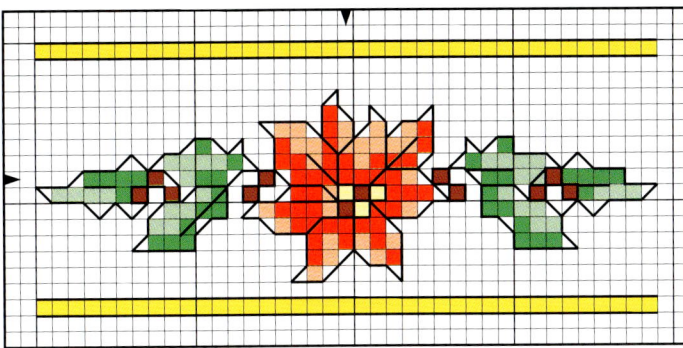

48

Design size: 39 wide x 17 high

Anchor	DMC
334	606
47	321
329	3340
301	744
311	676
206	564
208	563

Backstitch:
1005/816—flowers, berries
1048/3776—border
400/317—leaves

49

Design size: 96 wide x 42 high

Anchor	DMC	Anchor	DMC
2	blanc	328	3341
48	3689	311	676
50	3716	1042	504
54	956	875	503
334	606	216	502
47	321		

Backstitch:
59/326—pink flowers
1005/816—berries, remaining flower
218/319—leaves

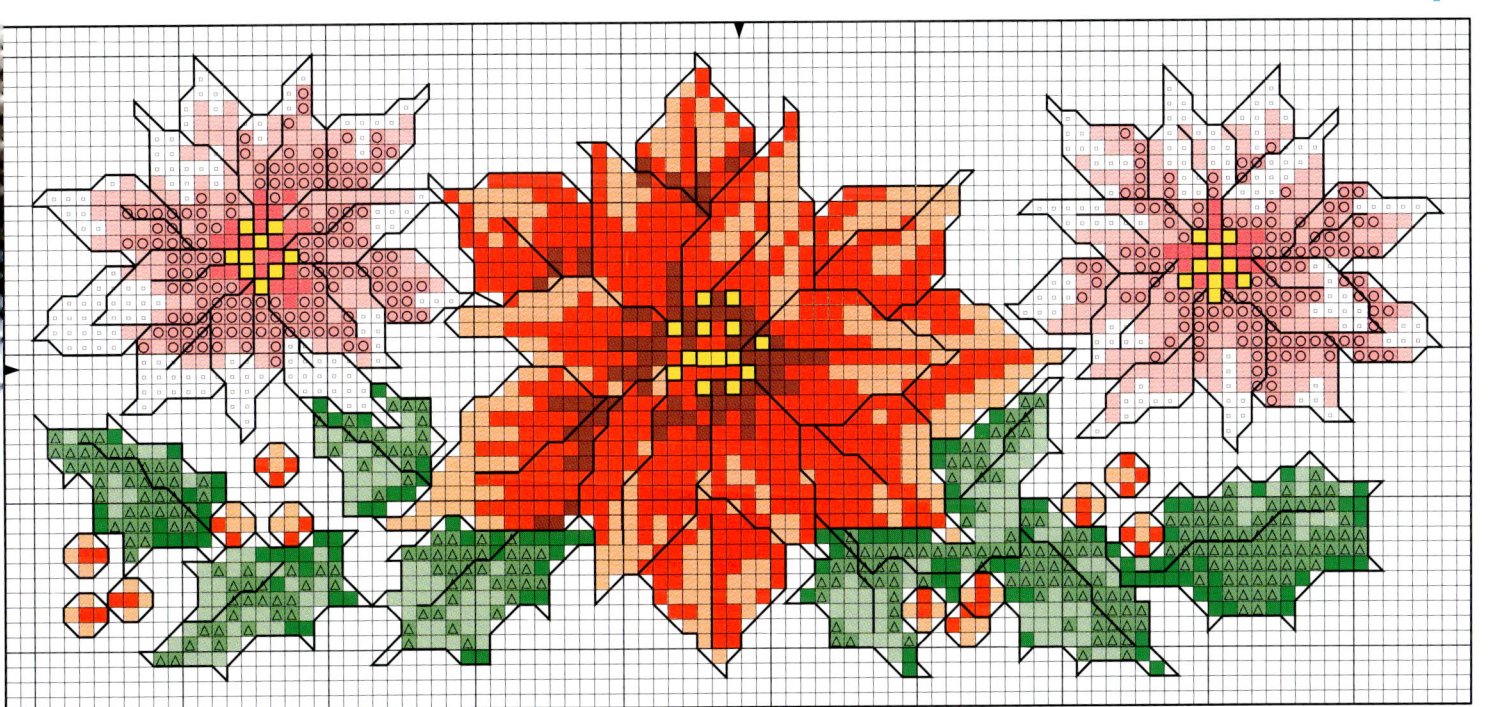

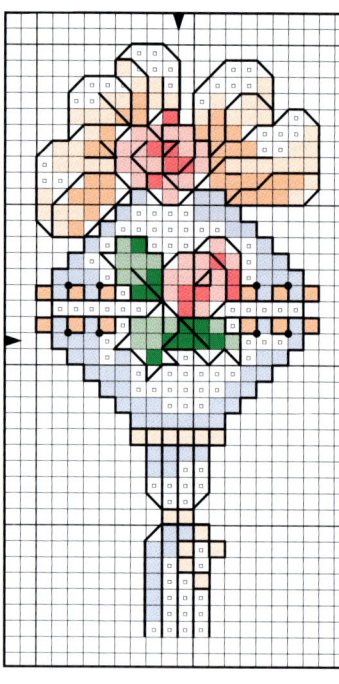

50

Design size: 18 wide x 37 high

Anchor	DMC
2	blanc
968	778
894	223
1012	754
868	758
213	504
859	523
128	775

French Knots: 1027/3722
Backstitch: 235/414

51

Design size: 20 wide x 37 high

Anchor	DMC
2	blanc
300	745
1012	754
868	758
301	744
311	676
302	743

French Knots: 338/922
Straight Stitch (bottom fringe): 1002/977
Backstitch: 400/317

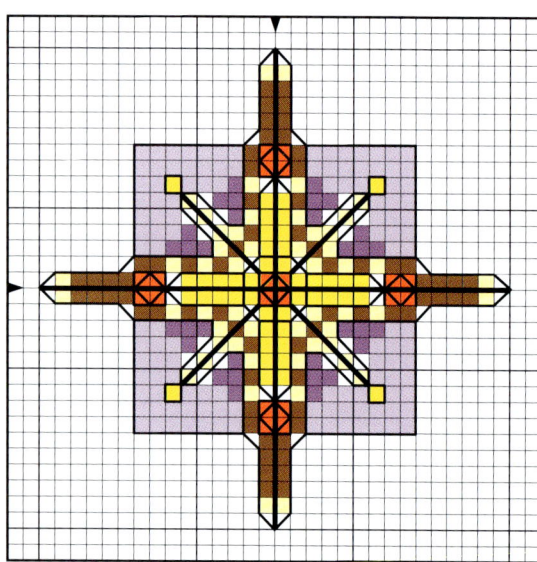

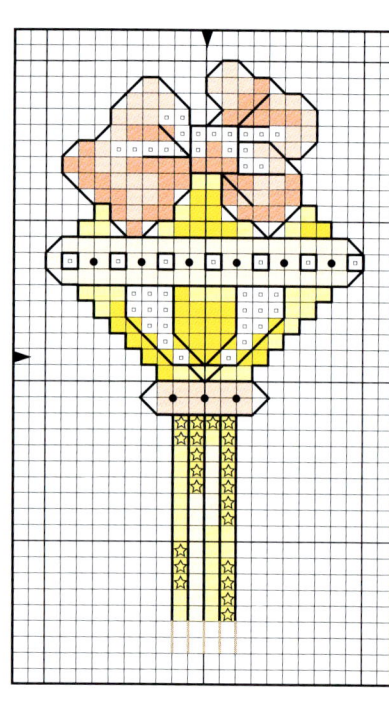

52

Design size: 30 wide x 30 high

Anchor	DMC
314	741
295	726
298	972
306	783
103	3609
90	554

Backstitch: 2/blanc (2 strands)—star
Backstitch:
309/781—remaining star
92/553—background square

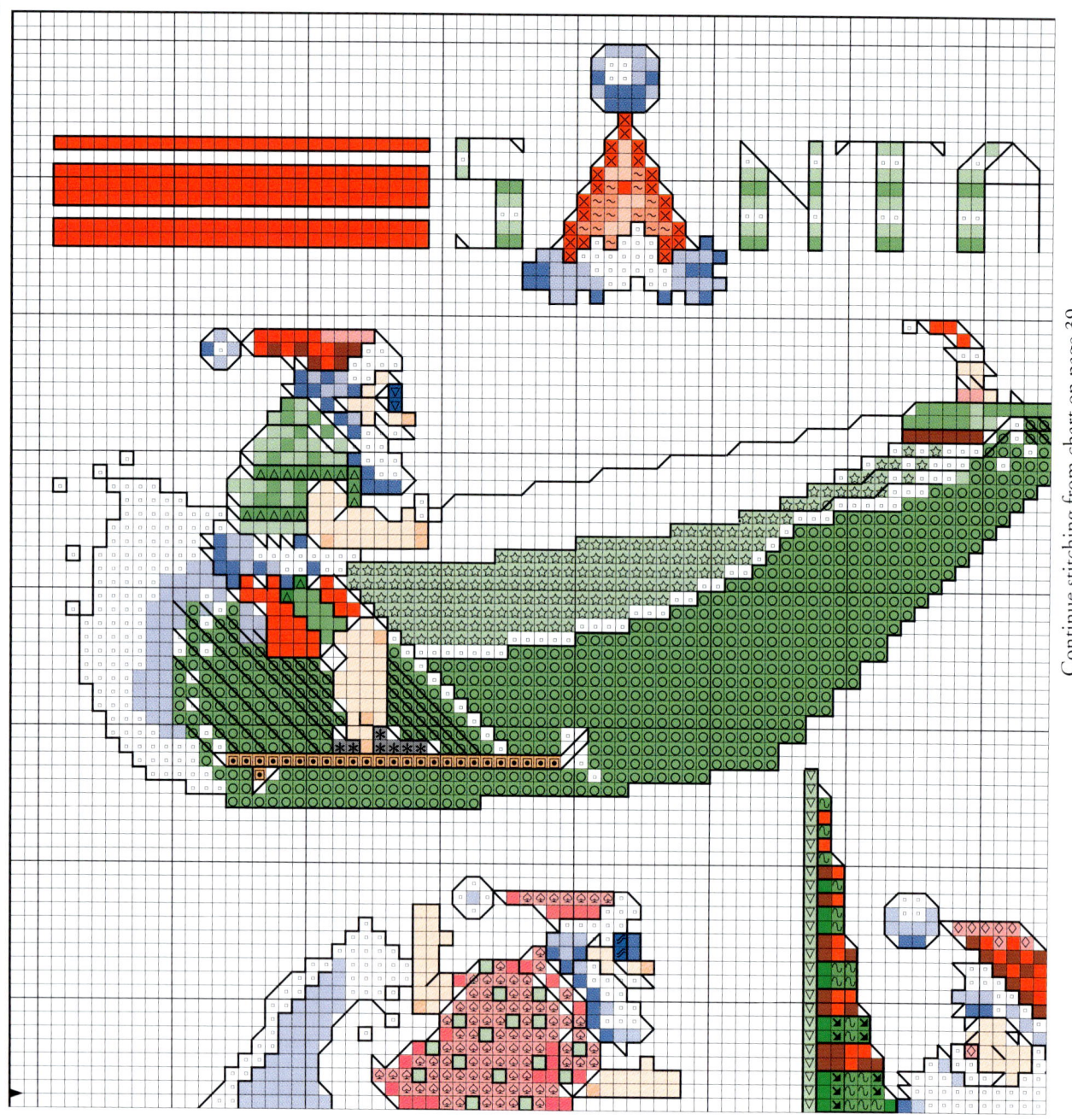

53–64 Sporty Santa Sampler

Design size: 174 wide x 154 high

Anchor	DMC	Anchor	DMC	Anchor	DMC	Anchor	DMC
2	blanc	13	347	9	352	1047	402
24	963	46	666	10	351	362	437
35	3705	47	321	314	741	1048	3776
38	961	778	3774	305	743	266	334
33	3706	868	758	311	742	262	3363
39	309	8	353	361	738	253	472

Continue stitching from chart on page 38

Continue stitching from chart on page 41

	Anchor	DMC		Anchor	DMC		Anchor	DMC		Anchor	DMC
▽	259	772	△	210	562		9159	3841		234	762
	225	703		226	703		160	827		398	415
☆	206	564		245	986		130	809	✱	399	318
◎	208	563	⊠	212	561		161	813		235	414
∼	254	907	∧	244	987		97	554	■	403	310
◉	238	703		186	959		884	356			
∪	240	966		128	775		347	402			

Color key continues on page 40

201 Cross-Stitch Christmas Designs • **39**

Continue stitching from chart on page 38

Continue stitching from chart on page 41

Color key begins on page 38

French Knots:
403/310—Biker's wheels
400/317—Fisherman's reel; Diver's belt, tank and glove

Backstitch:
2/blanc—"Santa" hat (except fur trims)
46/666—Sailor's shirt lines, border
20/815—"Santa" hat (except fur trims); Biker's hat and suit (except fur trims); Golfer's flag, socks, hat and jacket (except fur trims)
1006/304—Surfer's hat (except fur trims); Tennis Player's socks, hat and shirt (except fur trims)
1005/816—Water-skier's hats (except fur trims), pants; Baker's suit (except fur trims and belt); Sailor's shirt outlines, hat (except fur trims); Fisherman's hat and jacket (except fur trims); Kayaker's hat and coat (except fur trims); Boater's boat (except windshield and seat back), cap (except fur trims), coat
1025/347—Diver's hat and suit (except trims)
778/3774—Fisherman's skin
314/741—Water-skier's towline
305/743 (yellow)—Fisherman's lure and fly
306/783—Golfer's pole
262/3363—Fisherman's waders
211/562—Baker's mittens; Diver's green trims
212/561—"Santa" letters, Water-skier's life jacket, boat; green bike frame; Surfer's shirt, shorts; Sailor's sail, mast, pants; Tennis Player's shorts; Golfer's mittens, bag (except strap); Fisherman's mitten; Kayaker's trees, kayak; Boater's gift

Continue stitching from chart on page 39

Continue stitching from chart on page 40

Backstitch continued:
122/3807—Water-skier's glasses; Kayaker's water
978/322—"Santa" fur trims; Biker's, Baker's, Tennis Player's, Golfer's and Fisherman's fur trims, eyebrows, beards, mustaches; Surfer's fur trim, glasses, mustache, beard, water
161/813—Sailor's fur trims, beard, mustache, eyebrow, board; Kayaker's and Diver's fur trims, beards; Boater's fur trims, windshield, seat back; Water-skier's fur trims, beard, mustache, water, windshield

1039/518—Boater
99/552—surfboard
349/301—Water-skier's skin, ski (except boot); Tennis Player's skin, racket (except strings); Kayaker's paddle, skin, eye, eyebrow
883/3064—Sailor's skin, nose; Boater's face
884/356—Biker's nose, hand; Baker's nose and skin, rolling pin, belt buckle; Surfer's skin; Golfer's nose and skin, bag strap, belt buckle, pants, shoes (except spikes); Fisherman's nose, creel, rod

235/414—Biker's bike spokes, chain; Tennis Player's racket strings, shoes, eye; Golfer's eyes, clubs, shoe spikes
399/318—Baker's hat
400/317—Water-skier's ski boot, tow bar; Baker's eye, lettering, flour sack, boots, belt; Sailer's eyes, shoes; Fisherman's line, hook, reel; Diver's remaining outlines
403/310—Biker's remaining bike, boots, eyes; Golfer's belt

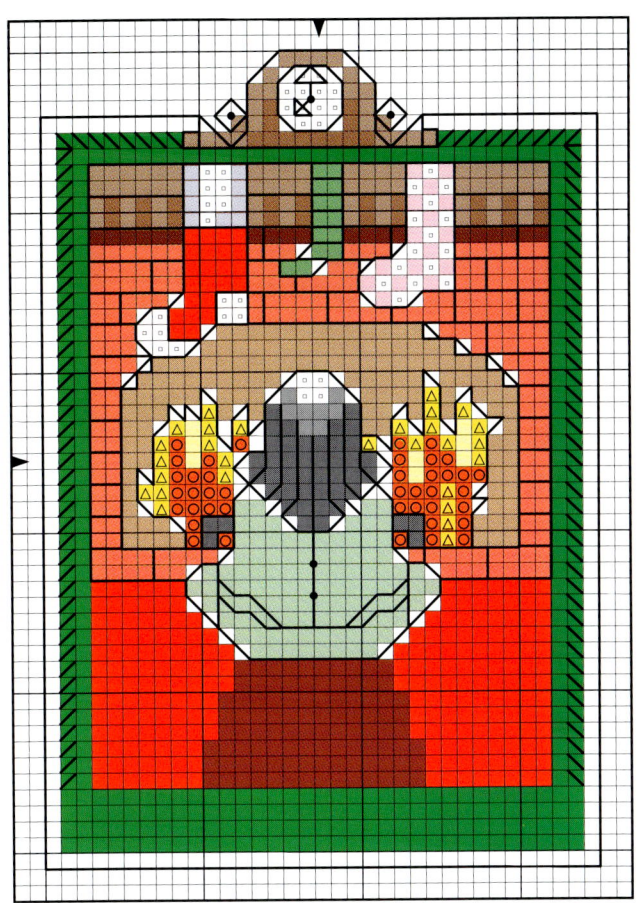

65

Design size: 35 wide x 51 high

Anchor	DMC
2	blanc
35	3705
46	666
1006	304
333	608
5975	356
301	744
303	742
890	729
1042	504
259	772
241	966
128	775
347	402
349	301
399	318
235	414

French Knots:
211/562—pajamas
349/301—clock finials
400/317—clock face

Backstitch:
1006/304—green stocking, stocking with white cuff, fire
211/562—remaining stocking, pajamas, border, background
349/301—clock (except hands), brown mantel
1015/3777—bricks
400/317—clock hands, hair, andirons

66

Design size: 44 wide x 52 high

Anchor	DMC
2	blanc
893	224
895	223
1027	3722
11	347
13	351
4146	950
882	758
1013	745
300	676
311	3855
1047	402
203	435
205	564
347	912
369	3778
398	415
235	414

French Knots: 236/3799

Backstitch:
47/321—red stocking stripes
211/562—green stocking stripes, pine branches
236/3799—remaining outlines

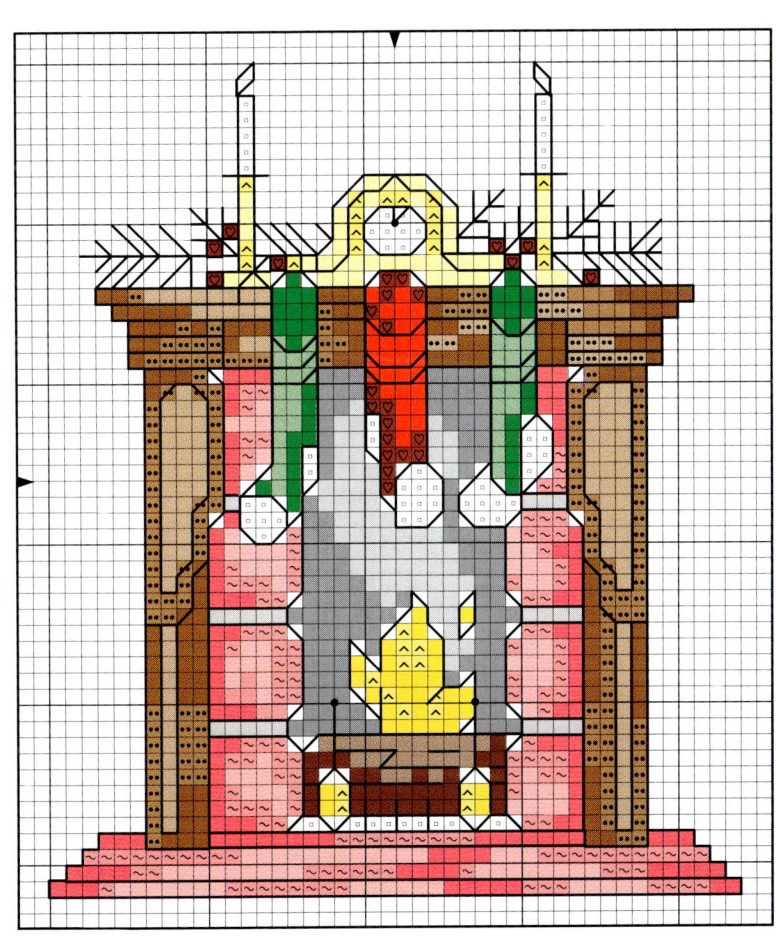

201 Cross-Stitch Christmas Designs • 43

67

Design size: 29 wide x 43 high

Anchor	DMC
13	347
10	351
313	742
293	727
311	676
875	503

Backstitch:
1002/977—tracery
217/561—frame
400/317—flame, candle

68

Design size: 48 wide x 44 high

Anchor	DMC
2	blanc
386	3823
894/895	224/223
1027	3722
9	352
11	351
1025	347
778	3774
300	745
311	676
366	951
368	437
214	368
216	502
129	809
136	799
109	209
370	434
399	318
400	317

French Knots:
13/347—wreath, tree
146/322—bridle, tree
400/317—horse's eye

Backstitch:
212/561—tree
1030/3746—lettering
400/317—remaining outlines

44 • 201 Cross-Stitch Christmas Designs

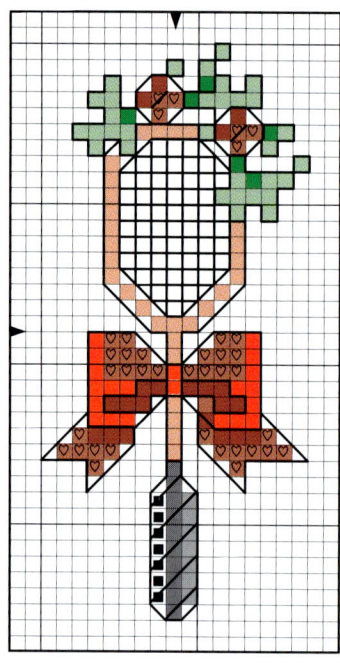

69

Design size: 17 wide x 36 high

	Anchor	DMC
	334	606
	47	321
	44	815
	226	703
	229	910
	1048	3776
	399	318
	236	3799
■	403	310

Backstitch:
2/blanc—berry highlights
44/815—berries, bow
229/910—leaves
403/310—racket

70

Design size: 32 wide x 32 high

	Anchor	DMC
	334	606
	47	321
	44	815
	226	703
	229	910
	399	318
	236	3799
■	403	310

Backstitch:
44/815—bow
229/910—leaves
403/310—club

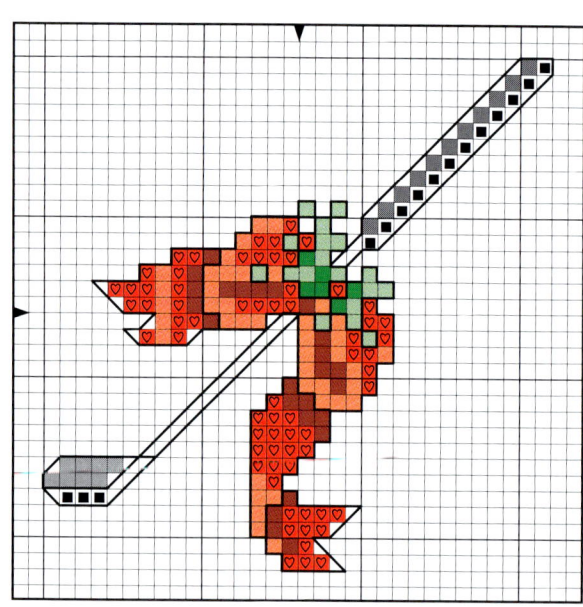

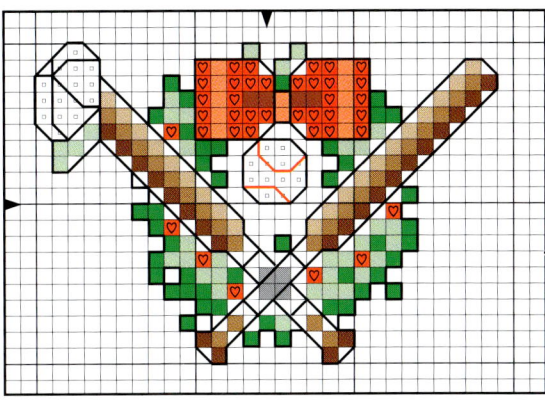

71

Design size: 29 wide x 20 high

Anchor	DMC
2	blanc
334	606
47	321
44	815
1047	402
1048	3776
226	703
229	910
351	400
399	318

Backstitch:
47/321—ball stitching
401/413—remaining outlines

72

Design size: 38 wide x 25 high

Anchor	DMC
2	blanc
334	606
47	321
44	815
226	703
229	910
923	699
1048	3776
1004	920
231	453

Backstitch:
44/815—bow
923/699—leaves
403/310—football

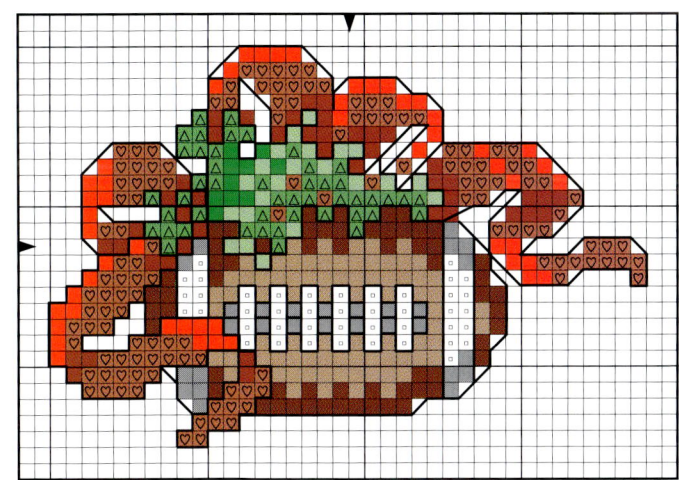

201 Cross-Stitch Christmas Designs • 47

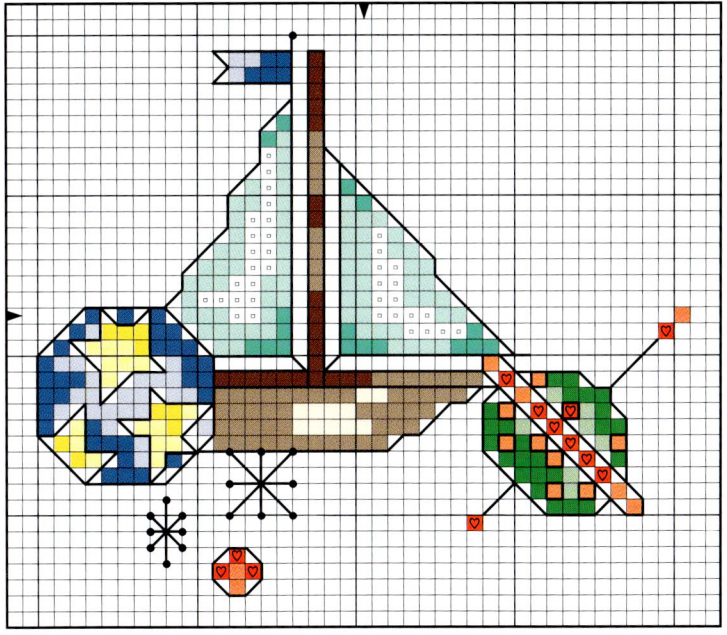

73

Design size: 41 wide x 35 high

Anchor	DMC
2	blanc
366	951
46	666
47	321
300	745
311	676
206	564
208	563
128	775
160	827
129	809
146	322
347	402
379	840

French Knots:
47/321—flag top
978/322—jacks

Eyelets (jacks): 978/322

Backstitch:
978/322—top spindle
400/317—remaining outlines

74

Design size: 25 wide x 31 high

Anchor	DMC
2	blanc
881	945
39	309
206	564
208	563

Backstitch:
2/blanc (2 strands)—sail stripes, birds
39/309—boat stripes, berries, inside boat
211/562—leaves
161/813—water
90/554—some clouds
108/210—remaining clouds
884/356—rope frame
921/931—remaining boat and sails

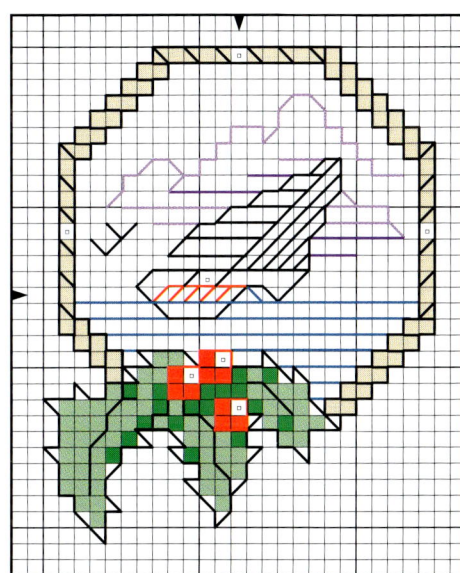

201 Cross-Stitch Christmas Designs • 49

75

Design size: 64 wide x 48 high

Anchor	DMC
334	606
314	741
241	966
161	813

French Knots: 42/326—anchor floats

Eyelets: 305/743—boat lights

Backstitch:
42/326—lighthouse, anchor
305/743 (yellow)—lighthouse light, light rays
211/562—lettering
161/813—water
92/553—clouds
884/356—cliffs
235/414—remaining outlines

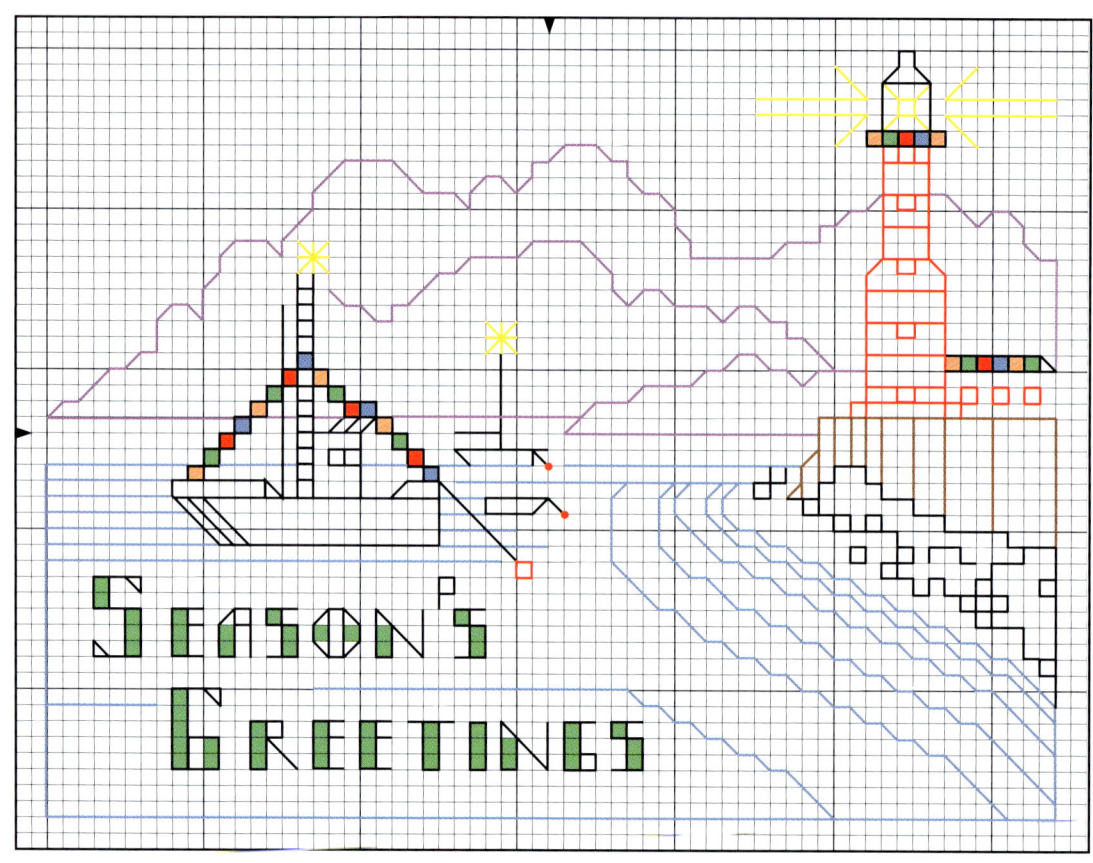

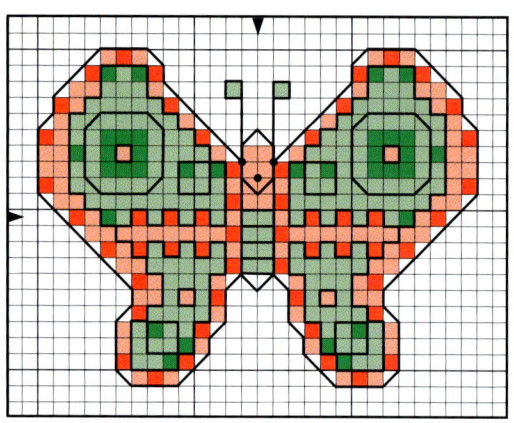

76

Design size: 28 wide x 21 high

Anchor	DMC
13	347
10	351
253	472
225	703

French Knots: 877/501

Backstitch:
20/815—wings, horizontal body stripes
877/501—remaining body, antennae

77

Design size: 28 wide x 22 high

Anchor	DMC
2	blanc
361	738
13	347
9	352
11	351
363	36
1031	3753
160	827
336	402

French Knots: 20/815

Backstitch:
20/815—pig, hat (except trim)
978/322—hat fur trim, eyes

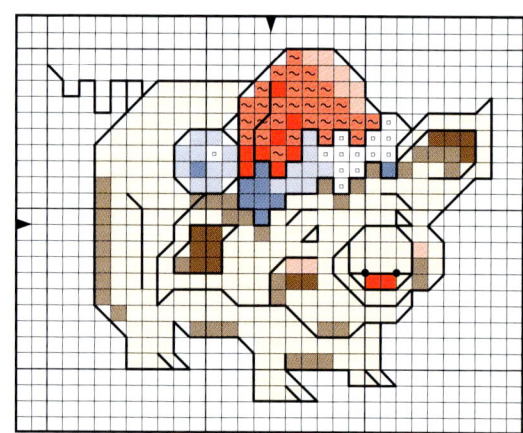

78

Design size: 38 wide x 37 high

Anchor	DMC
24	963
26	894
39	309
47	321
10	351
301	744
311	676
1002	977
206	564
875	503
876	502

French Knot: 400/317

Backstitch:
878/501—leaves
400/317—remaining outlines

79

Design size: 36 wide x 26 high

Anchor	DMC
2	blanc
36	3326
38	961
39	309
206	564
208	563

Backstitch:
43/814—lettering, berries
212/561—leaves

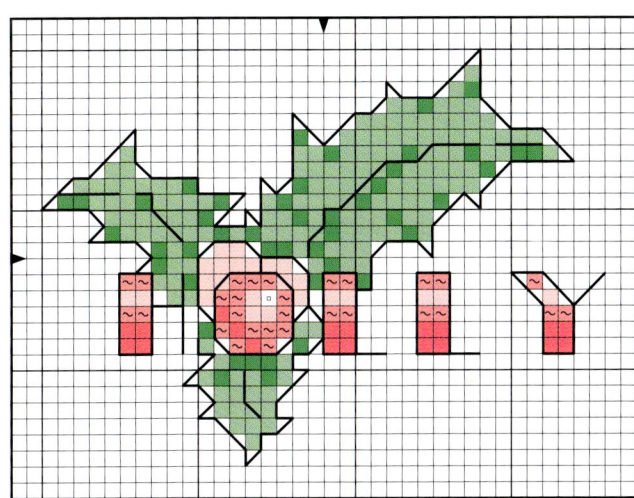

54 • 201 Cross-Stitch Christmas Designs

80

Design size: 77 wide x 18 high

Anchor	DMC
8	353
10	351
13	347

Backstitch: 20/815

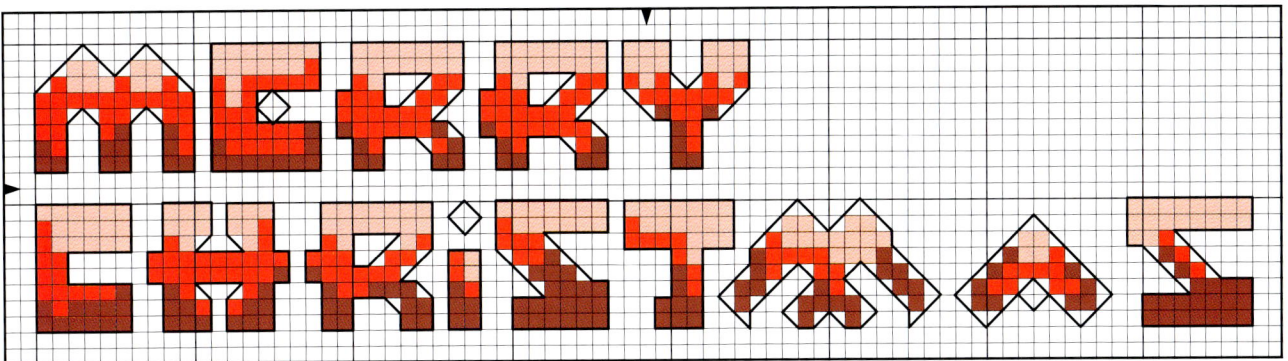

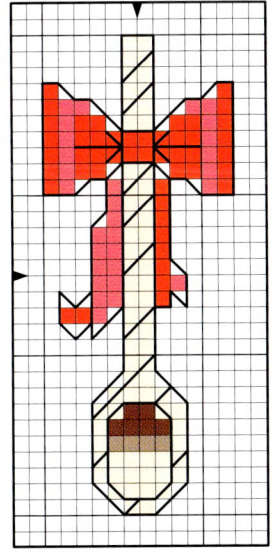

81

Design size: 12 wide x 30 high

Anchor	DMC
4146	950
33	3706
1098	3801
882	758
883	3064

Backstitch:
47/321—bow
884/356—spoon

82

Design size: 17 wide x 54 high

Anchor	DMC
2	blanc
334	606
47	321
44	815
226	703
229	910
142	798
1048	3776
403	310

Backstitch: 403/310

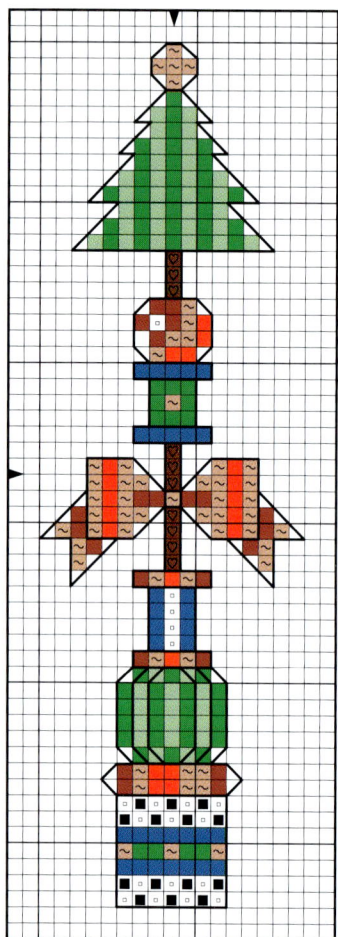

83

Design size: 19 wide x 51 high

Anchor	DMC
2	blanc
334	606
47	321
44	815
314	741
326	720
302	743
226	703
229	910
923	699
1048	3776
231	453
403	310

Backstitch: 403/310

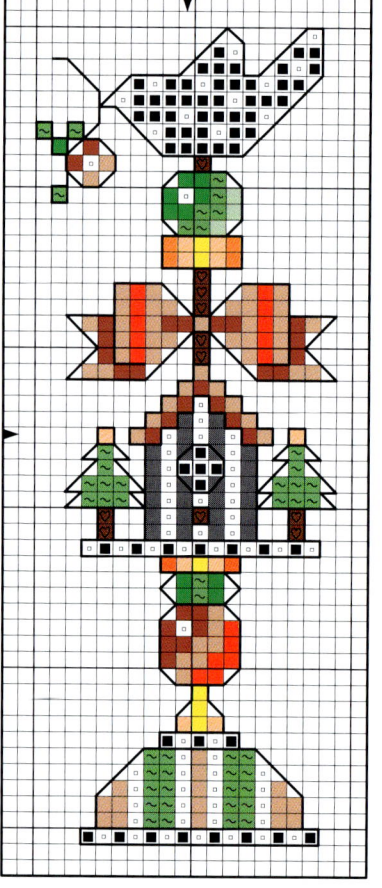

56 • *201 Cross-Stitch Christmas Designs*

84

Design size: 65 wide x 14 high

	Anchor	DMC
○	2	blanc
	11	351
	13	347
	301	744
	203	564
	128	775

French Knots: 47/321

Backstitch:
210/562—leaves, pine needles
136/799—flowers
400/317—ribbon, yellow buds

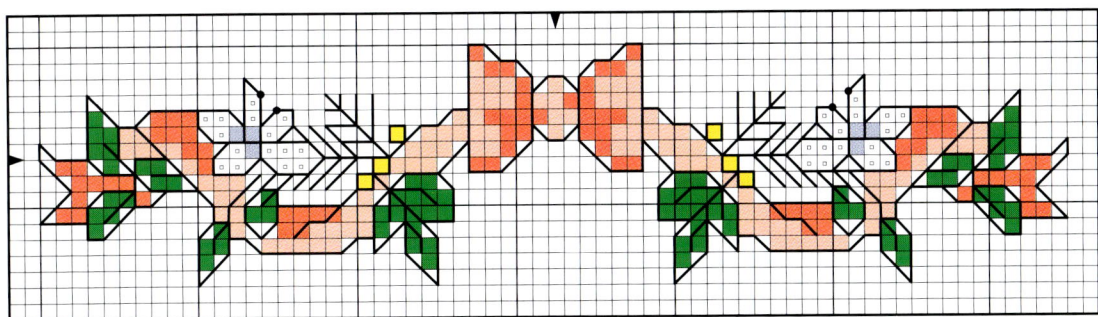

85

Design size: 35 wide x 13 high

	Anchor	DMC
○	2	blanc
	323	722
	128	775
	160	827
	399	318
	400	317

Backstitch:
333/608—nose
161/813—letters
403/310—snowman's eyes, eyebrows and mouth
400/317—remaining snowman

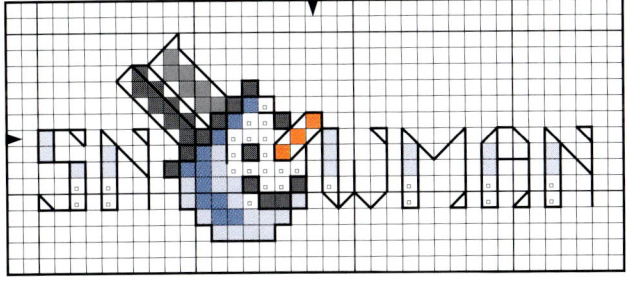

201 Cross-Stitch Christmas Designs • 57

86

Design size: 99 wide x 42 high

Anchor	DMC
27	899
334	606
1006	304
329	3340
301	744
1002	977
259	772
265	3347
258	905
1049	301
403	310

Backstitch:
2/blanc—berries
351/400—letter "M", branch, scroll
1005/816—red cardinal edges (except beak), berries, tracery, remaining lettering
246/986—leaves
403/310—remaining cardinal

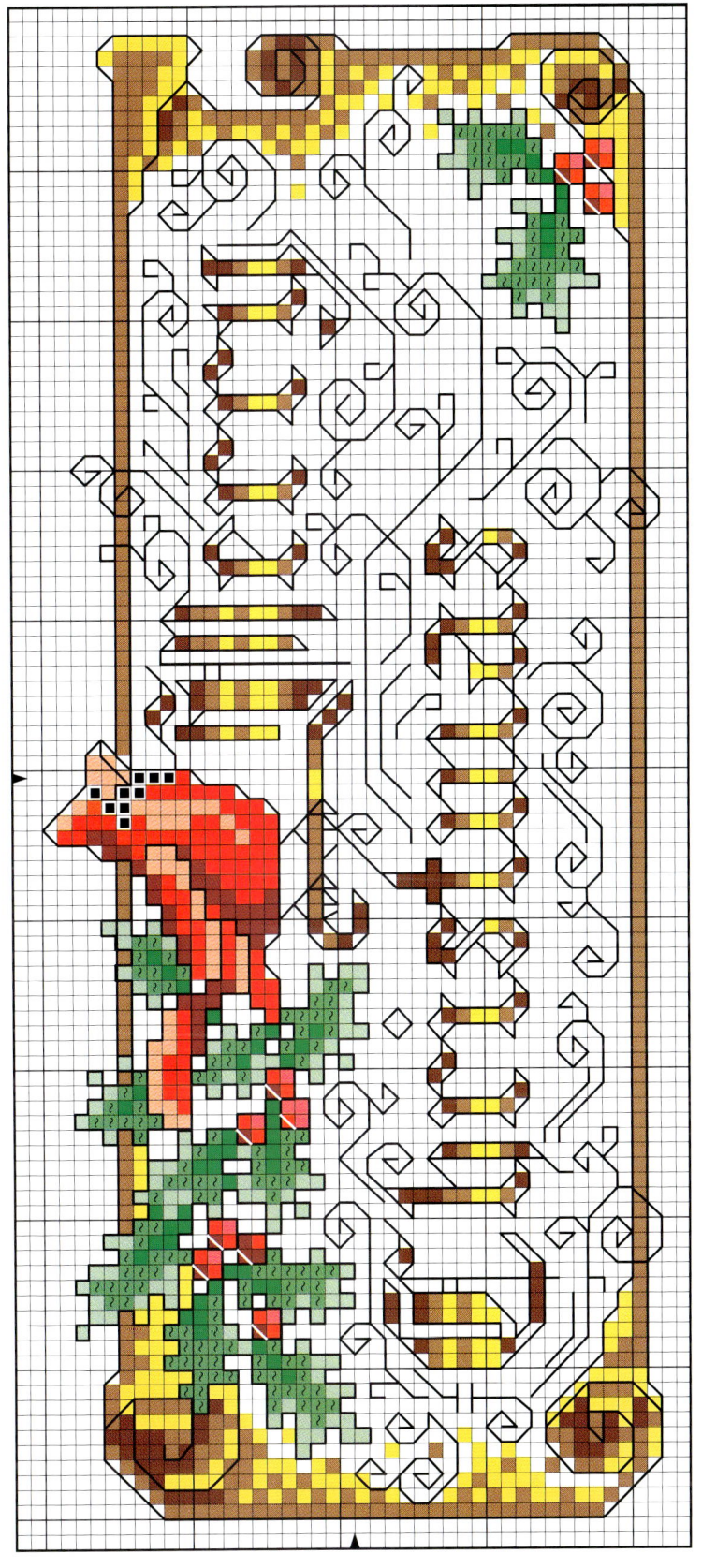

201 Cross-Stitch Christmas Designs • 59

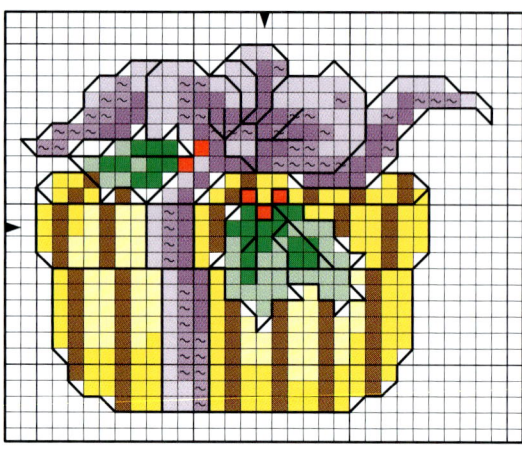

87

Design size: 30 wide x 23 high

	Anchor	DMC
■	47	321
	300	745
	311	676
	347	402
	206	564
	208	563
	342	211
	108	210
	109	209

Backstitch: 400/317

88

Design size: 40 wide x 24 high

	Anchor	DMC
■	47	321
	882	758
	300	745
~	301	744
	311	676
	206	564
	208	563
	342	211
	109	209
	883	3064

Backstitch:
877/501—pine needles
884/356—apples and pear (except stems)
400/317—remaining outlines

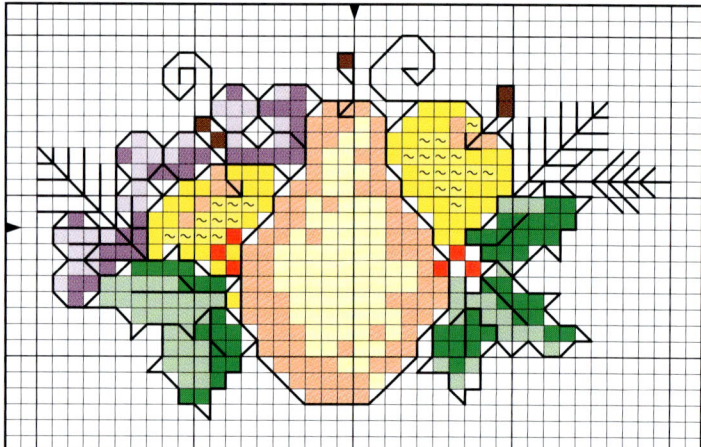

89

Design size: 37 wide x 22 high

	Anchor	DMC
	2	blanc
■	46	666
	323	722
	259	3348
	254	368
	264	772
~	266	3347
	217	561
	1031	3753
	129	809

French Knots: 936/632

Backstitch: 936/632—stems

Backstitch:
20/815—buds
267/469—light green leaves
217/561—remaining leaves
922/930—roses

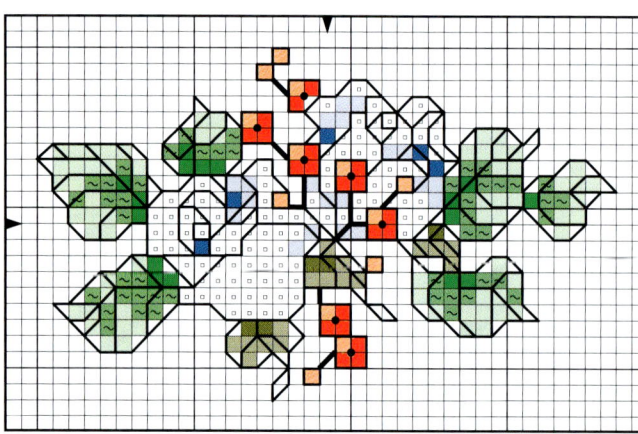

60 • *201 Cross-Stitch Christmas Designs*

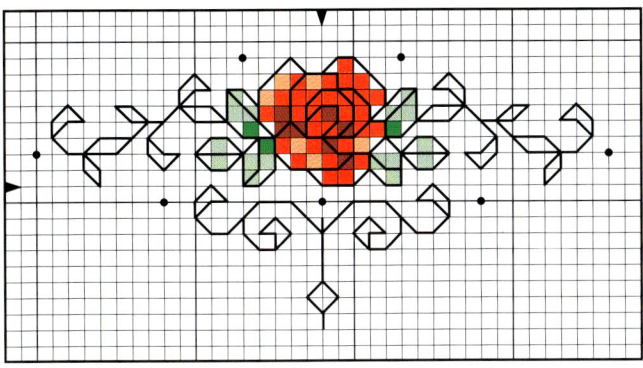

90

Design size: 36 wide x 18 high

Anchor	DMC
46	666
47	321
328	3341
209	913
878	501

French Knots: 878/501

Backstitch:
20/815—rose
307/783—design
878/501—leaves

91

Design size: 38 wide x 33 high

Anchor	DMC
2	blanc
24	963
778	3774
882	758
883	3064
292	3078
311	676
302	743
1042	504
875	503
261	989
1031	3753
936	632

Backstitch (2 strands):
883/3064—skin
862/520—green collar
1007/3772—hair, cream collar
936/632—eyes, nose
399/318—wings

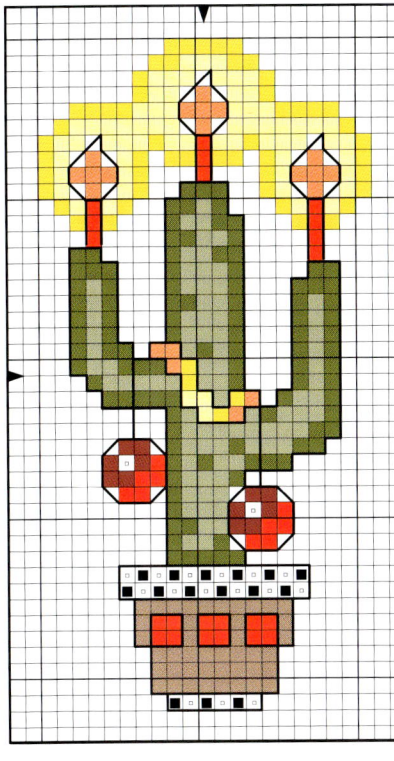

92

Design size: 21 wide x 42 high

	Anchor	DMC
▫	2	blanc
■	9046	666
■	1005	816
■	314	741
■	300	745
■	302	743
■	842	3013
■	843	3053
■	338	922
■	403	310

Backstitch:
44/815—candles, ornaments
326/720—flames, garland
845/730—cactus, ornament hangers, pot spots
403/310—remaining pot

93

Design size: 36 wide x 40 high

	Anchor	DMC
▫	2	blanc
■	54	956
■	9046	666
■	1005	816
■	314	741
■	324	721
■	302	743
■	226	703
■	229	910
■	167	519
■	168	807
■	169	806
■	1048	3776

Backstitch:
1005/816—garland, red wheel edge
923/699—tree, handle knob, remaining wheel
169/806—candles, cart (except handle)
1048/3776—star, flames, tree trunk, cart handle

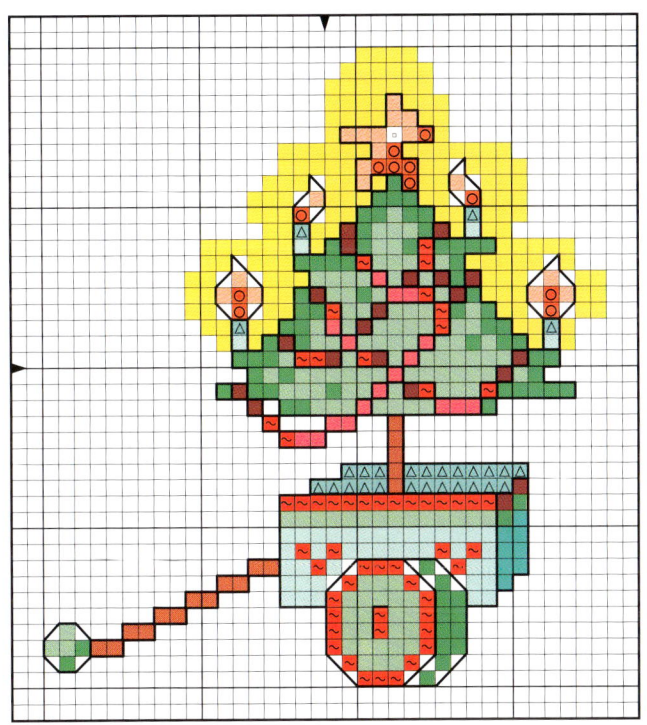

94

Design size: 23 wide x 44 high

Anchor	DMC
2	blanc
334	606
47	321
44	815
226	703
229	910
923	699
1048	3776
231	453
233	451

Backstitch: 401/413

95

Design size: 26 wide x 26 high

Anchor	DMC
2	blanc
13	347
10	351
778	3774
241	966
159	3325
160	827
234	762

Eyelets (stars): 11/351

Backstitch:
11/351—mouth
13/347—hat (except fur trim), suit, "Christmas"
211/562—"Merry"
161/813—fur trim, beard, eyes, eyebrows
921/931—life preserver

64 • *201 Cross-Stitch Christmas Designs*

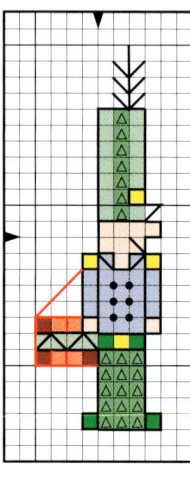

96

Design size: 8 wide x 24 high

Anchor	DMC
46	666
47	321
778	3774
302	743
253	472
241	966
210	562
928	3761

French Knots: 302/743

Backstitch:
1005/816—drum (except center band)
302/743—feather
217/561—center drum band, uniform, hat
1007/3772—skin

97

Design size: 12 wide x 30 high

Anchor	DMC
2	blanc
46	666
778	3774
868	758
314	741
161	813
234	762
399	318

French Knots: 401/413

Backstitch:
2/blanc (2 strands)—button chains
314/741—feather
401/413—remaining outlines

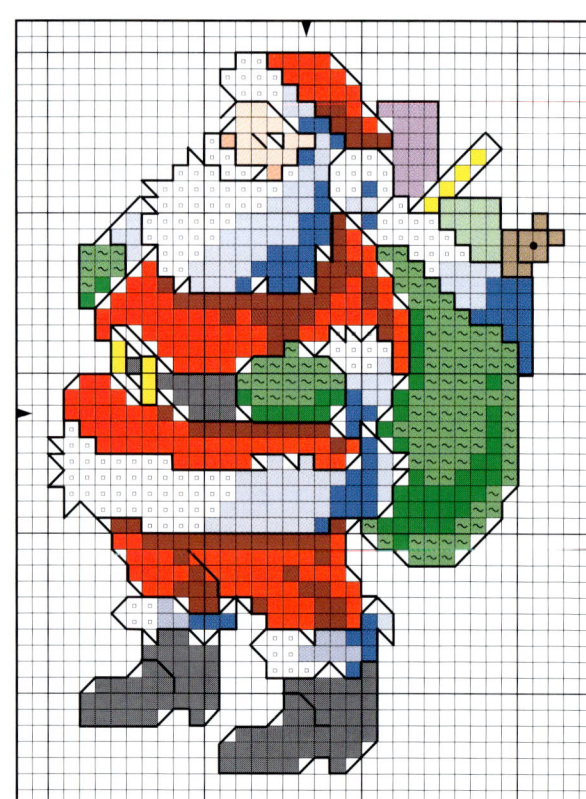

98

Design size: 33 wide x 45 high

Anchor	DMC
2	blanc
46	666
47	321
778	3774
8	353
302	743
206	564
240	966
243	703
128	775
160	827
96	3609
347	402
399	318

French Knot: 351/400

Backstitch:
47/321—suit and hat (except fur trims)
212/561—mittens, bag, green present
99/552—purple present, stick
351/400—bear
921/931—beard, mustache, eyebrows, fur trims
400/317—eyes, belt, boots

66 • 201 Cross-Stitch Christmas Designs

99

Design size: 38 wide x 29 high

	Anchor	DMC	Backstitch:
	2	blanc	47/321—fireplace sides, flames
	361	738	210/562—garland
	29	309	99/552—stockings, lights, andirons
	46	666	
	330	947	355/975—remaining fireplace, clock, logs
	303	742	
	363	436	
	253	472	
	241	966	
	185	964	
	161	813	
	347	402	
	1049	301	
	399	318	

100

Design size: 20 wide x 35 high

	Anchor	DMC
	2	blanc
	1025	347
	10	351
	313	742
	240	966
	225	703
	1032	3752
	161	813
	347	402

French Knots: 401/413

Eyelet (star): 302/743

Backstitch:
302/743—beak
211/562—tree
146/322—icicles, lights
349/301—clock (except face and hands)
401/413—face, hands, remaining bird

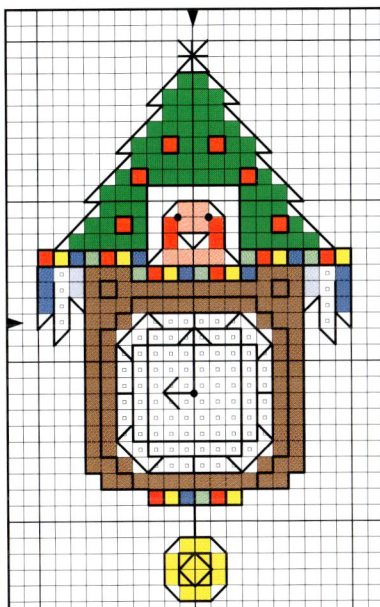

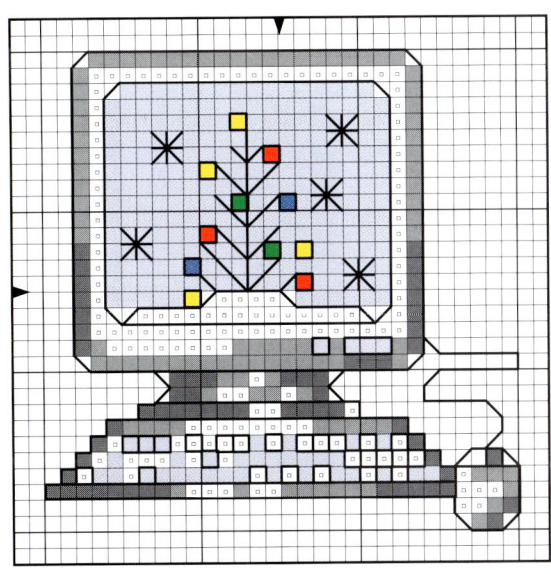

101

Design size: 30 wide x 30 high

	Anchor	DMC
	2	blanc
	46	666
	302	743
	253	472
	128	775
	136	799
	234	762
	399	318

Eyelets (snowflakes): 136/799

Backstitch:
217/561—tree
136/799—snow
401/413—remaining outlines

201 Cross-Stitch Christmas Designs • 67

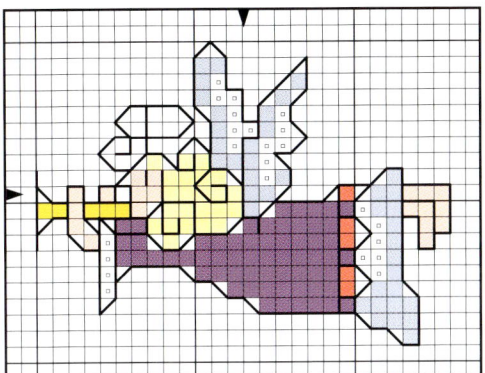

102

Design size: 26 wide x 19 high

Anchor	DMC
2	blanc
778	3774
9	352
301	744
313	742
128	775
118	340

Backstitch:
302/743 (2 strands)—halo
369/435 (2 strands)—hair, eye
400/317—remaining outlines

103

Design size: 37 wide x 21 high

Anchor	DMC
2	blanc
300	745
46	666
47	321
301	744
311	676
1002	977
253	472
225	703
210	562
185	964
160	827
121	809

Backstitch:
2/blanc (2 strands)—smoke
305/743 (2 strands)—light rays
1002/977—engine, smoke stack, bell
111/208—train

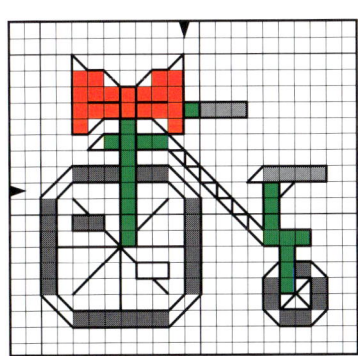

104

Design size: 18 wide x 17 high

Anchor	DMC
35	3705
238	703
234	762
399	318

Backstitch:
47/321—bow
244/987—frame
400/317—reamining outlines

201 Cross-Stitch Christmas Designs • 69

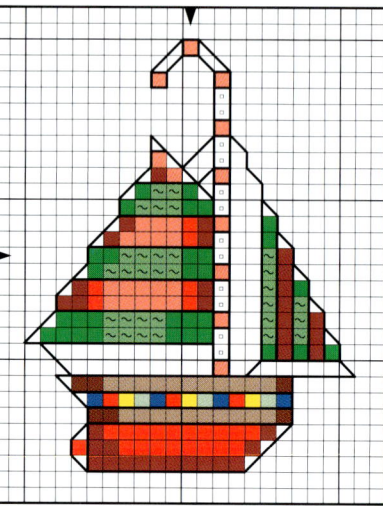

105

Design size: 21 wide x 27 high

Anchor	DMC
2	blanc
1098	3801
13	347
11	351
314	741
240	966
225	703
244	987
161	813
347	402
349	301

Backstitch:
47/321—candy cane mast
217/561—remaining outlines

106

Design size: 14 wide x 29 high

Anchor	DMC
2	blanc
40	956
42	326
323	722
301	744
302	743
225	703
128	775
235	414

Backstitch (2 strands):
42/326—H's
225/703—wreath needles
212/561—remaining wreath
978/322—snowman face outline
884/356—top ornament
400/317—remaining snowman

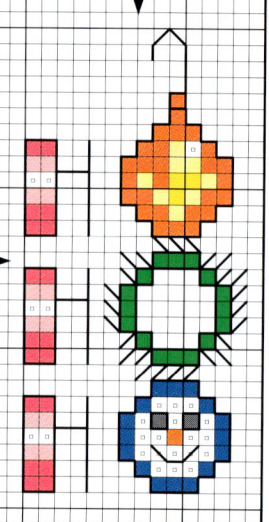

107

Design size: 17 wide x 23 high

Anchor	DMC
2	blanc
38	961
39	309
778	3774
253	472
225	703
210	562
212	561
128	775
160	827

French Knots: 978/322

Backstitch:
1006/304—hat, mittens and boots (except fur trims)
212/561—ornament
978/322—fur trims
1013/3778—skin

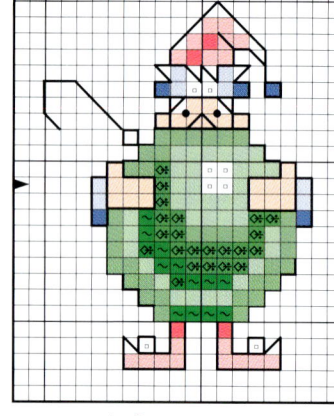

108

Design size: 14 wide x 23 high

Anchor	DMC
33	3706
1098	3801
778	3774
241	966
209	913
210	562
128	775
129	809

French Knots: 137/798

Backstitch:
47/321—hat (except trim), ribbon
211/562—box, shoes
137/798—hat trim, cuffs
883/3064—face, hands, eyebrows

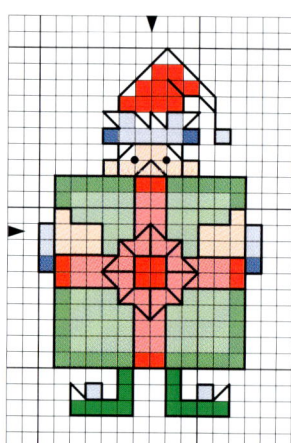

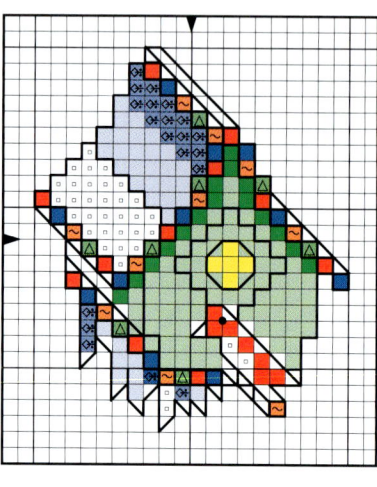

109

Design size: 20 wide x 24 high

Anchor	DMC
2	blanc
19	304
314	741
293	727
206	564
238	703
205	912
1032	3752
160	827
161	813

French Knot: 162/825

Backstitch:
19/304—bird
162/825—icicles, lightest blue top edge of roof
211/562—remaining outlines

110

Design size: 20 wide x 24 high

Anchor	DMC
2	blanc
46	666
96	3609
778	3774
238	703
244	987
128	775
160	827
342	211

French Knots:
1006/304—box decoration
99/552—eyes

Backstitch:
1006/304—hat (except fur trims), box decoration
212/561—remaining box
99/552—fur trims, shirt, mittens and face
883/3064—skin

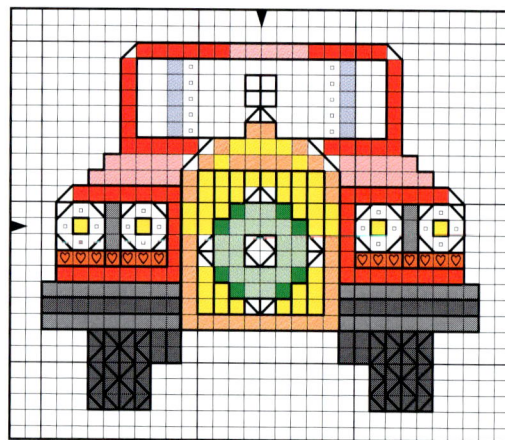

111

Design size: 28 wide x 23 high

Anchor	DMC
2	blanc
33	3706
1098	3801
314	741
925	947
311	676
238	703
227	701
1032	3752
234	762
399	318

Backstitch:
47/321—car (except grill lines, bumpers, lights)
314/741—hood ornament
217/561—wreath
235/414—grill lines, bumpers, lights
400/317—tires

72 • *201 Cross-Stitch Christmas Designs*

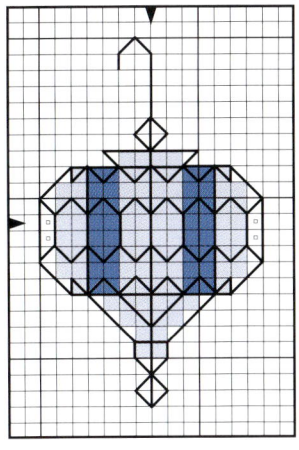

112

Design size: 14 wide x 23 high

Anchor	DMC
2	blanc
1090	996
117	341

Backstitch (2 strands):
2/blanc—center line
122/3807—ornament
400/317—hanger

113

Design size: 10 wide x 26 high

Anchor	DMC
2	blanc
342	211
96	3609

Backstitch (2 strands):
2/blanc—center line
111/208—ornament
98/553—hanger

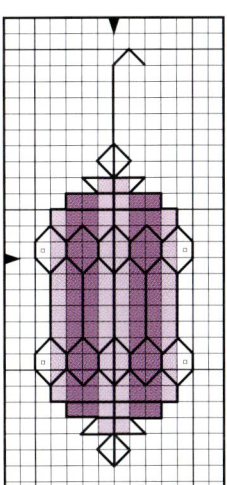

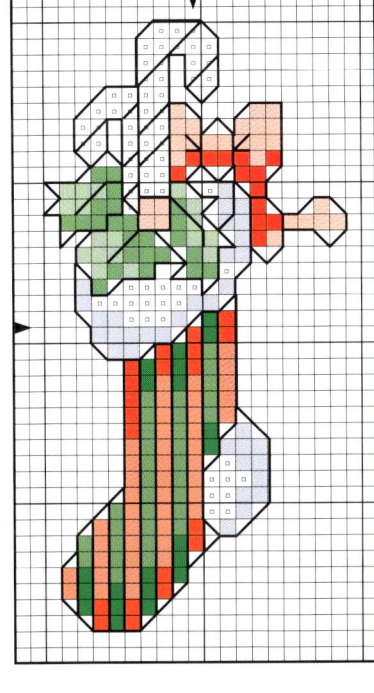

114

Design size: 19 wide x 38 high

Anchor	DMC	Backstitch:
2	blanc	1025/347—bow, candy canes
1025	347	212/561—leaves
1024	3328	400/317—stocking
11	351	
206	564	
208	563	
210	562	
128	775	

201 Cross-Stitch Christmas Designs • 73

74 • 201 Cross-Stitch Christmas Designs

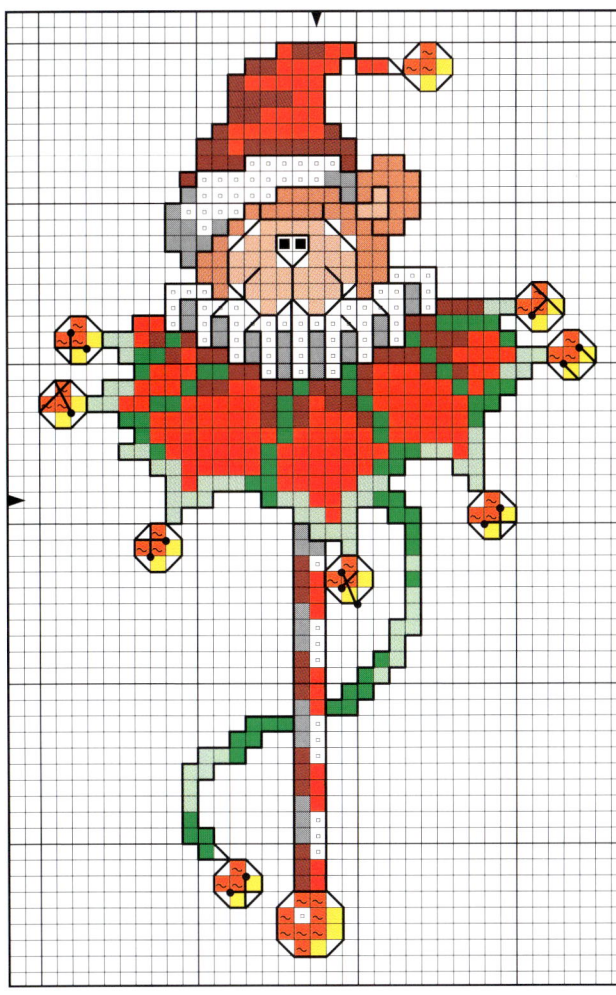

115

Design size: 35 wide x 57 high

Anchor	DMC
2	blanc
9046	666
1005	816
314	741
302	743
226	703
229	910
1047	402
1048	3776
231	453
403	310

French Knots: 403/310

Backstitch:
1005/816—red hat edges, stick
923/699—green color edges, ribbon
351/400—hat ornament, bells (except slits), bear (except face), stick knob
403/310—remaining edges

116

Design size: 38 wide x 59 high

Anchor	DMC
2	blanc
50	3716
9046	666
1005	816
314	741
326	720
302	743
226	703
229	910
923	699
231	453
403	310

French Knots: 403/310

Backstitch:
1005/816—berry, stick
923/699—leaves, green collar, ribbons
351/400—gold collar edges, bells (except slits), stick knob
403/310—remaining outlines

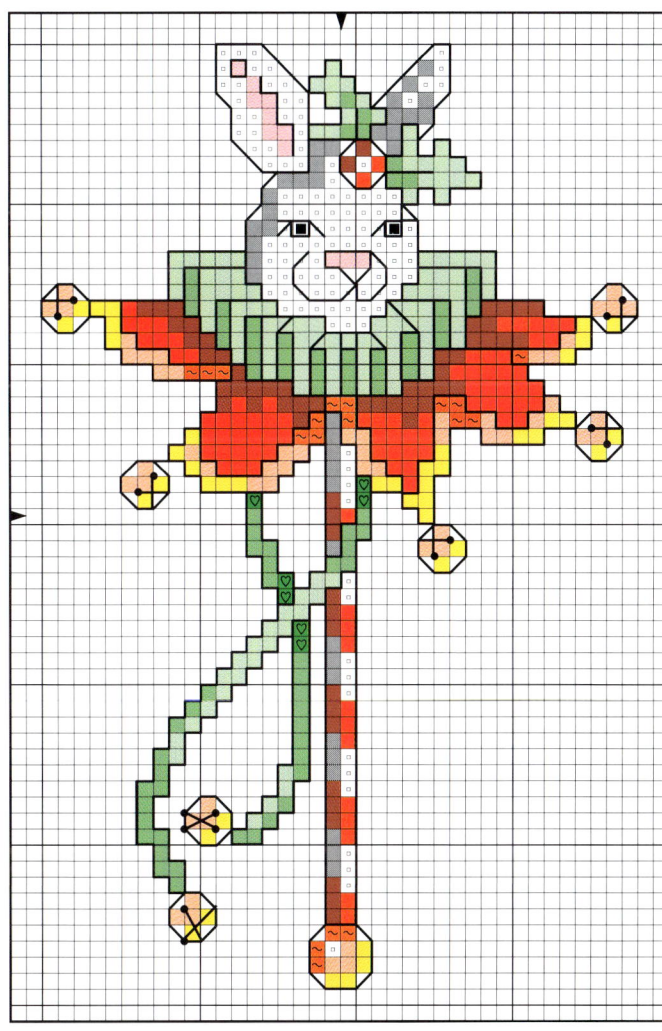

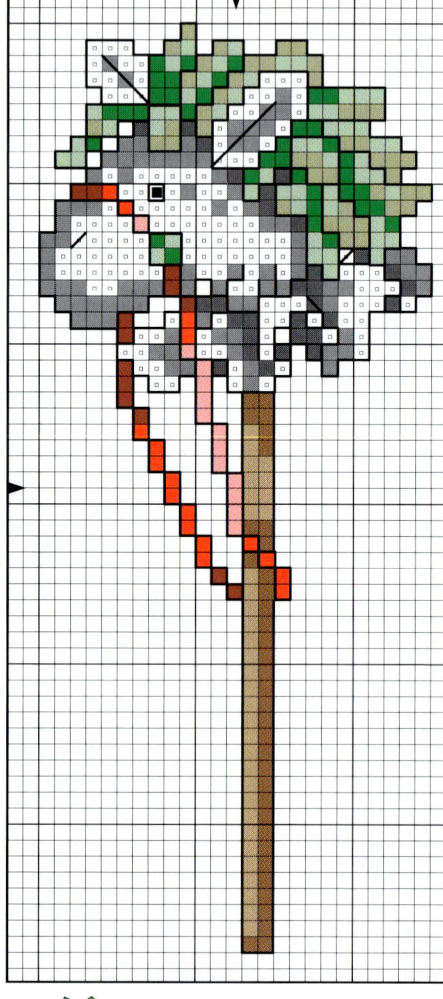

117

Design size: 25 wide x 58 high

Anchor	DMC
2	blanc
54	956
9046	666
1005	816
363	436
255	907
257	905
246	986
1048	3776
231	453
233	451
403	310

Backstitch:
1005/816—halter
683/816—mane, bit
1004/920—stick
403/310—remaining outlines

118

Design size: 45 wide x 54 high
Stitching note: use one strand white to work a very small French Knot for eye highlight.

Anchor	DMC
2	blanc
47	321
44	815
314	741
326	720
302	743
226	703
229	910
142	798
139	797
231	453
233	451
403	310

French Knots: 403/310

Backstitch:
44/815—berry, red saddle trim
923/699—leaves, green straps
351/400—pole, bell (except slits)
403/310—remaining outlines

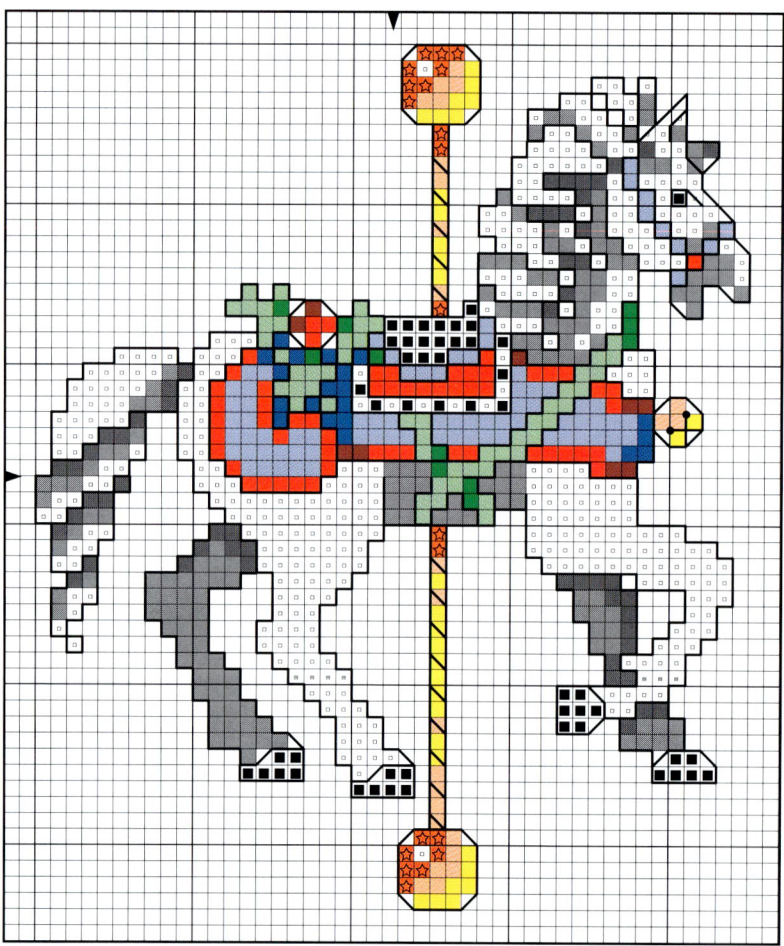

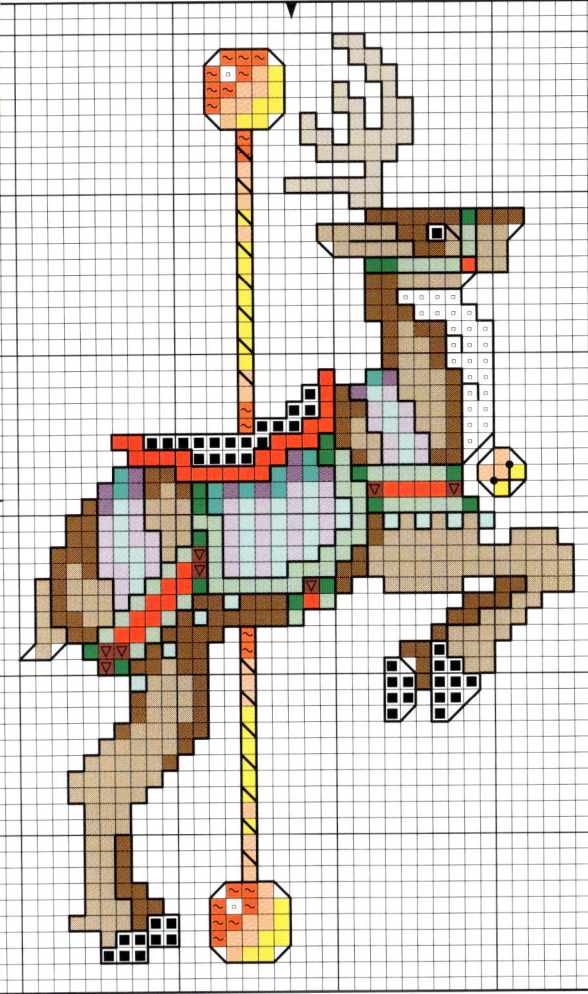

119

Design size: 35 wide x 58 high

Anchor	DMC
2	blanc
47	321
44	815
314	741
326	720
302	743
1047	402
1048	3776
226	703
229	910
1070	993
1074	992
108	210
110	208
903	640
403	310

French Knots: 403/310

Backstitch:
229/910—bridle, green saddle strap and strap edges
112/552—purple strap edges, tassels
351/400—pole, bell (except slits)
403/310—remaining outlines

120

Design size: 44 wide x 58 high
Stitching note: use one strand white to work a very small French Knot for eye highlight.

Anchor	DMC
2	blanc
47	321
314	741
326	720
302	743
226	703
142	798
1047	402
1048	3776
903	640
403	310

Backstitch:
44/815—red saddle and strap trim
351/400—pole
403/310—remaining outlines

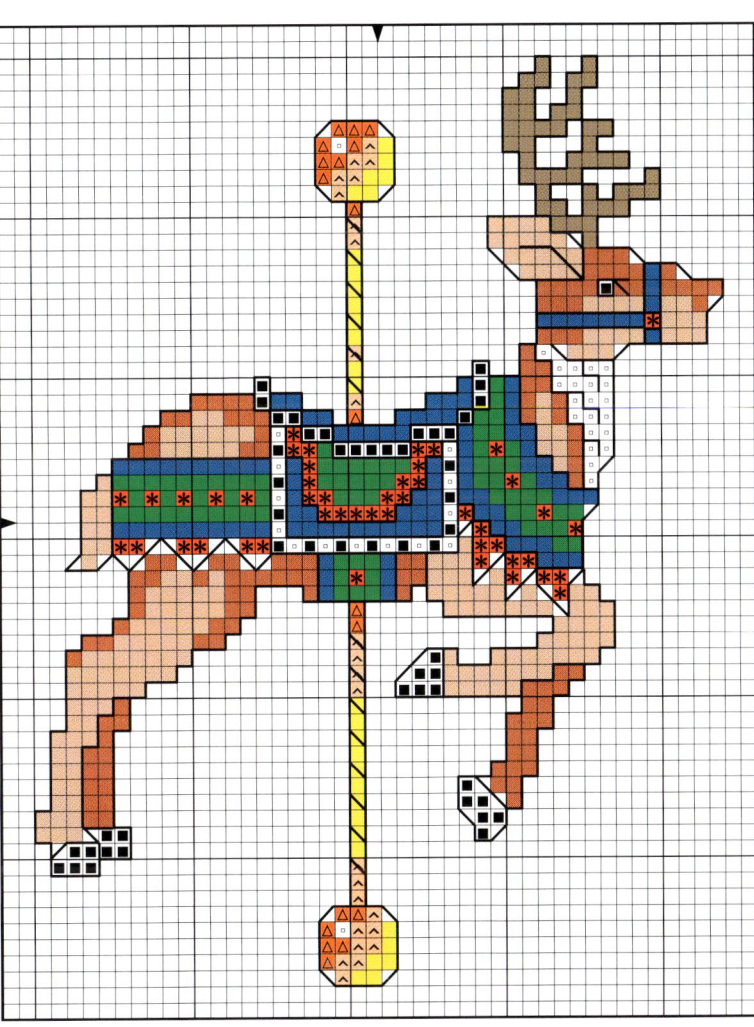

201 Cross-Stitch Christmas Designs • 77

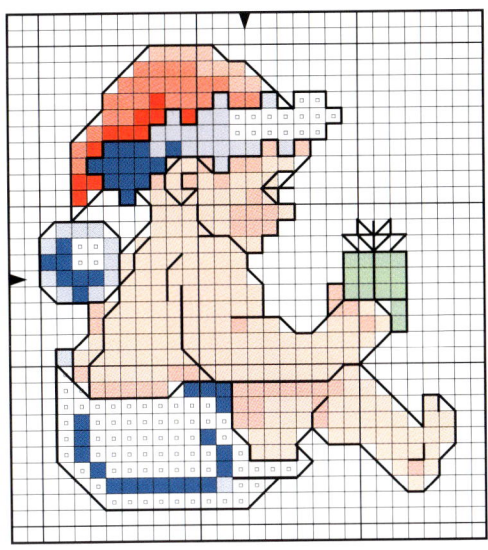

121

Design size: 26 wide x 29 high

Anchor	DMC
2	blanc
13	347
778	3774
9	352
11	351
203	564
1031	3753
160	827

Backstitch:
20/815—hat (except trim)
978/322—hat trim, gift, diaper
883/3064—baby

122

Design size: 23 wide x 37 high

Anchor	DMC
2	blanc
36	3326
13	347
778	3774
868	758
10	351
1031	3753
160	827

French Knots: 883/3064

Backstitch:
20/815—hat (except trim)
978/322—hat trim, diaper
883/3064—baby

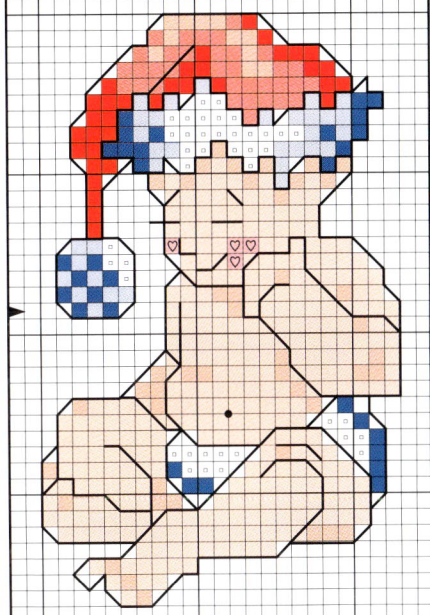

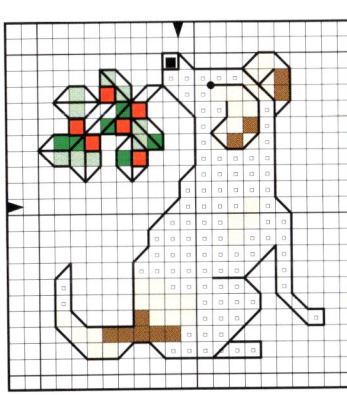

123

Design size: 18 wide x 19 high
Stitching note: three strands used for cross-stitches.

Anchor	DMC
2	blanc
372	738
46	666
374	420
254	3348
256	704

French Knot (2 strands): 403/310

Backstitch (3 strands):
1006/304—berries
944/434—dog (except nose)
211/562—leaves
403/310—nose

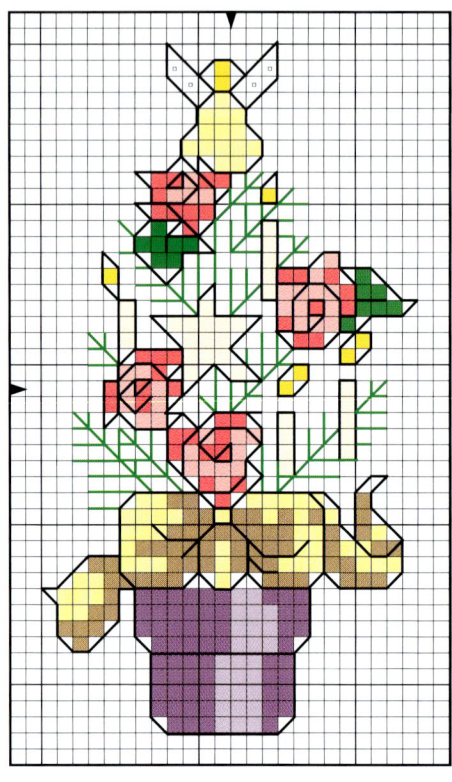

124

Design size: 24 wide x 43 high

Anchor	DMC
2	blanc
300	745
27	899
29	309
301	744
311	676
1002	977
875	503
342	211
109	209

Backstitch:
877/501—branches
400/317—remaining oulines

125

Design size: 31 wide x 32 high

Anchor	DMC
2	blanc
24	963
46	666
778	3774
301	744
311	676
261	989
217	561
1031	3753
976	3752
977	334
979	312
376	3774
378/379	841/840
403	310

French Knots: 403/310

Backstitch:
2/blanc—cuff and collar stripes
1005/816—mittens, berries
979/312—clothes
379/840—skin, hair
936/632—snowman's hat, pipe, branches
235/414—snow
403/310—boots, snowman's eyes and buttons

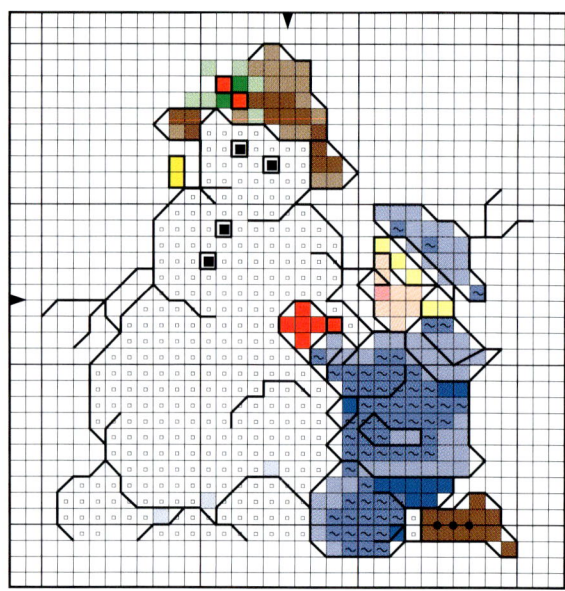

126

Design size: 30 wide x 30 high

Anchor	DMC
2	blanc
46	666
47	321
20	815
323	722
264	3348
266	3347
217	561

Anchor	DMC
160	827
161	813
979	312

Backstitch:
20/815—roses
217/561—leaves, stems
979/312—ribbon

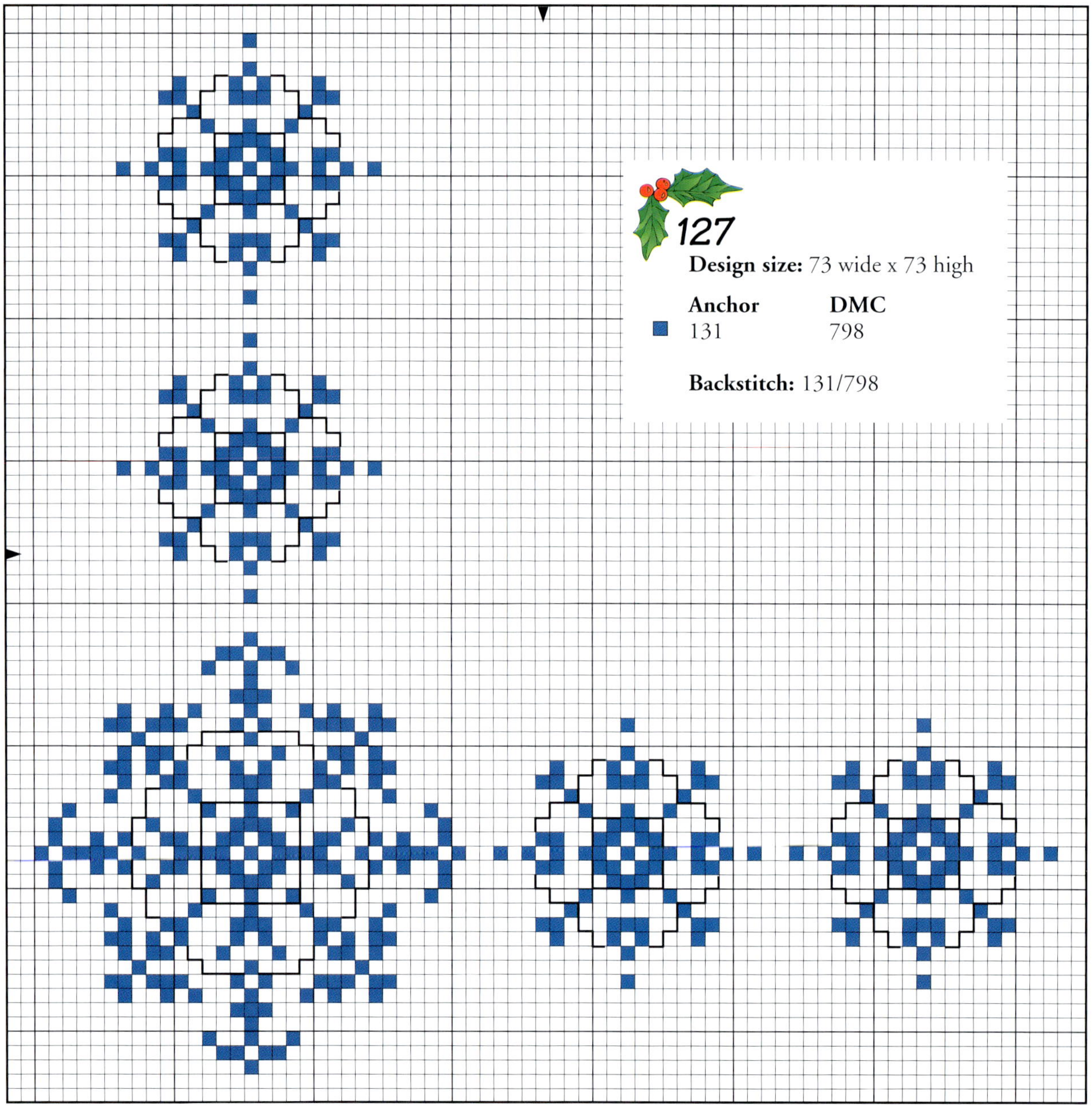

127

Design size: 73 wide x 73 high

Anchor	DMC
131	798

Backstitch: 131/798

82 • 201 Cross-Stitch Christmas Designs

128

Design size: 27 wide x 39 high

Anchor	DMC
2	blanc
334	606
47	321
44	815
314	741
326	720
302	743
1047	402
1048	3776
226	703
229	910
137	798
903	640
403	310

French Knots: 403/310

Backstitch:
701 (muliné lamé)—light cord, lights
403/310—remaining outlines

129

Design size: 25 wide x 38 high

Anchor	DMC
2	blanc
11	351
13	347
253	472
225	703
128	775
109	209
110	208
401	413

French Knot: 401/413

Straight Stitch:
225/703—scarf fringe

Backstitch:
145/809—snow, pole
401/413—remaining outlines

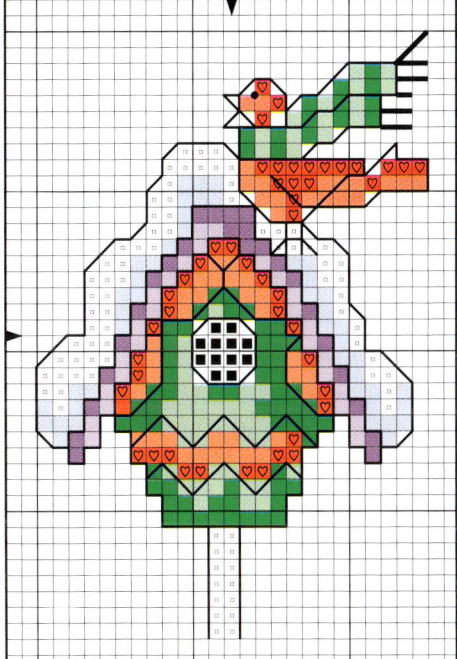

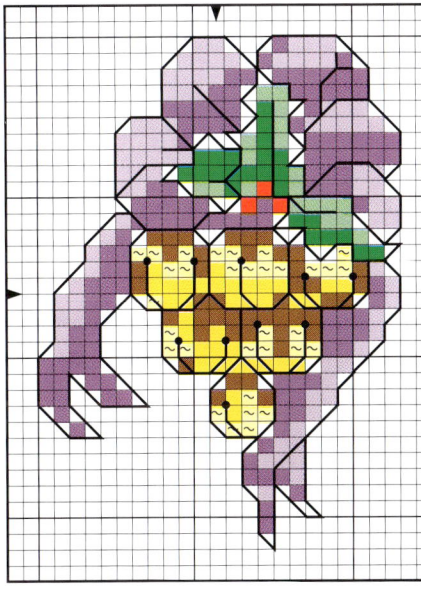

130

Design size: 23 wide x 32 high

Anchor	DMC
46	666
300	745
311	676
313	742
241	966
243	703
117	341
118	340

French Knots: 401/413

Backstitch:
211/562—leaves
401/413—remaining outlines

201 Cross-Stitch Christmas Designs • 83

 **131**

Design size: 21 wide x 25 high

Anchor	DMC
2	blanc
885	739
1021	761
1025	347
46	666
1015	3777
361	738
264	3348
266	3347
217	561

French Knots: 46/666

Backstitch:
46/666—string, label lines, holly berries
1015/3777—tomatoes
217/561—leaves
235/414—jar, label outline (except lettering)
403/310—lettering

 **132**

Design size: 24 wide x 25 high

Anchor	DMC
2	blanc
46	666
47	321
1005	816
323	722
311	676
1002	977
234	762

Backstitch:
1005/816—ribbon, berry
1049/301—lettering
210/562—pine needles
235/414—jar
403/310—label

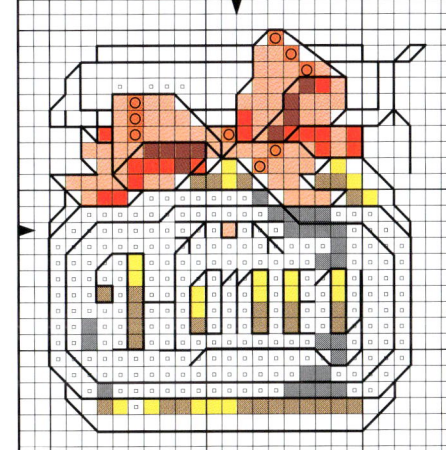

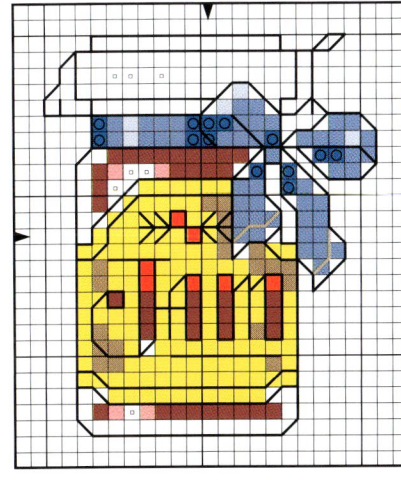

 **133**

Design size: 21 wide x 25 high

Anchor	DMC
2	blanc
76	961
46	666
43	814
311	676
1047	402
128	775
130	809
979	312

Backstitch:
43/814—label, berries, lettering
311/676—bow stripes
210/562—pine needles
979/312—ribbon
235/414—jar

201 Cross-Stitch Christmas Designs • 85

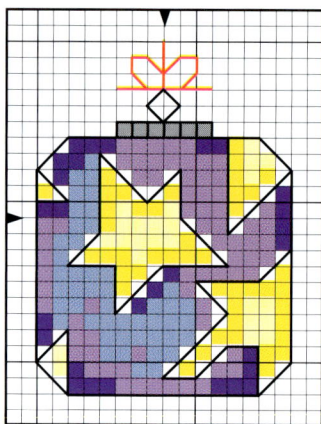

134

Design size: 73 wide x 24 high

Anchor	DMC
129	809
118	340

Backstitch: 119/333

135

Design size: 16 wide x 22 high

Anchor	DMC
301	744
302	743
176	793
1030	3746
119	333
234	762

Backstitch:
46/666—bow
401/413—remaining outlines

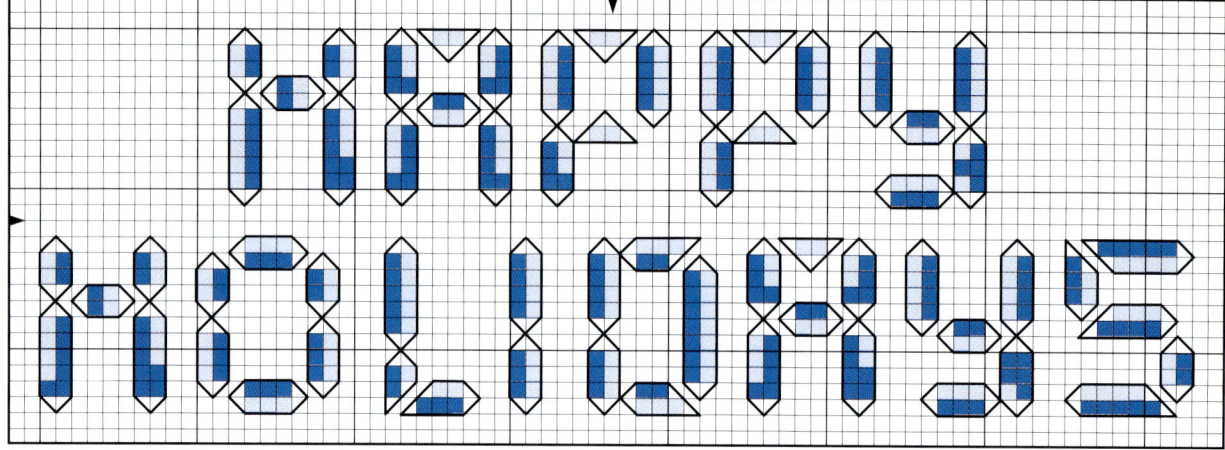

136

Design size: 14 wide x 20 high

Anchor	DMC
301	744
302	743
234	762

French Knots: 46/666

Backstitch:
46/666—swirl, bow
226/703—swirls
1030/3746—swirls
401/413—remaining outlines

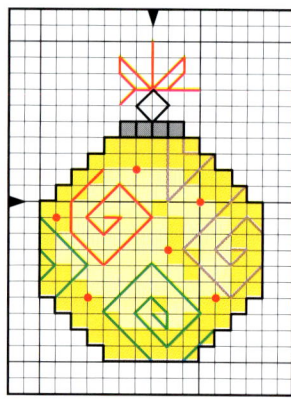

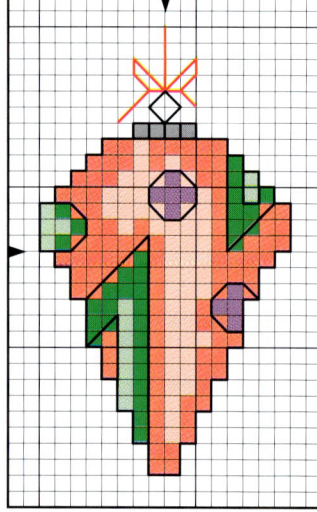

137

Design size: 16 wide x 28 high

Anchor	DMC
9	352
11	351
253	472
225	703
118	340
234	762

Backstitch:
46/666—bow
401/413—remaining outlines

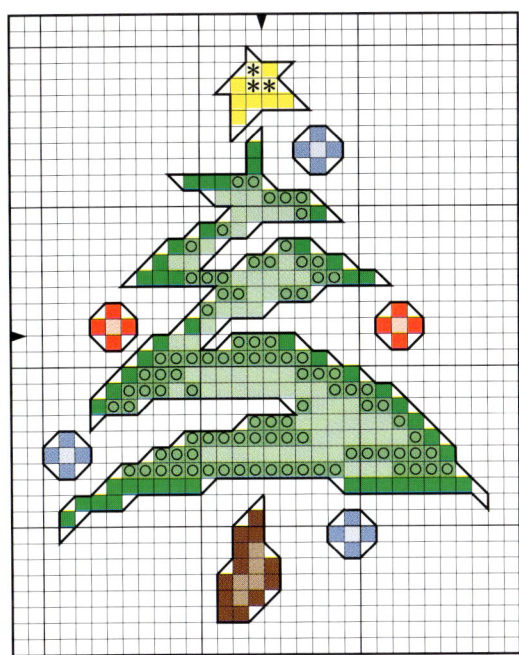

138

Design size: 28 wide x 36 high

Anchor	DMC
13	347
10	351
301	744
302	743
206	564
208	563
217	561

Anchor	DMC
160	827
977	334
376	3774
379	840

Backstitch: 400/317

139

Design size: 32 wide x 29 high

Anchor	DMC
9	352
11	351
13	347
301	744
311	676
313	742

Backstitch:
936/632—stars
401/413—ribbon

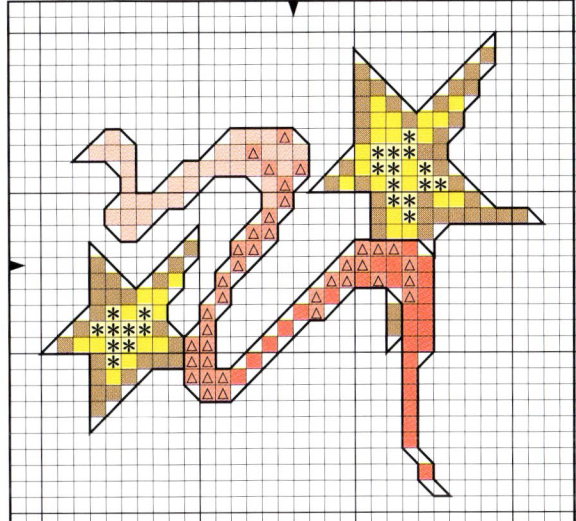

140

Design size: 46 wide x 23 high

Anchor	DMC
885	739
13	347
9	352
11	351
206	564
208	563
128	775
160	827
161	813
117	341
118	340
398	415
235	414
400	317

French Knots: 400/317
Backstitch: 400/317

141

Design size: 24 wide x 35 high

Anchor	DMC
2	blanc
334	606
47	321
44	815
314	741
326	720
302	743
226	703
229	910
923	699
1048	3776
231	453
403	310

Backstitch: 403/310

142

Design size: 21 wide x 53 high

Anchor	DMC	Anchor	DMC
2	blanc	226	703
334	606	229	910
47	321	923	699
44	815	1048	3776
314	741	403	310
324	721		
326	720		
300	745		
302	743		

French Knot: 923/699

Backstitch:
923/699—lettering
403/310—remaining outlines

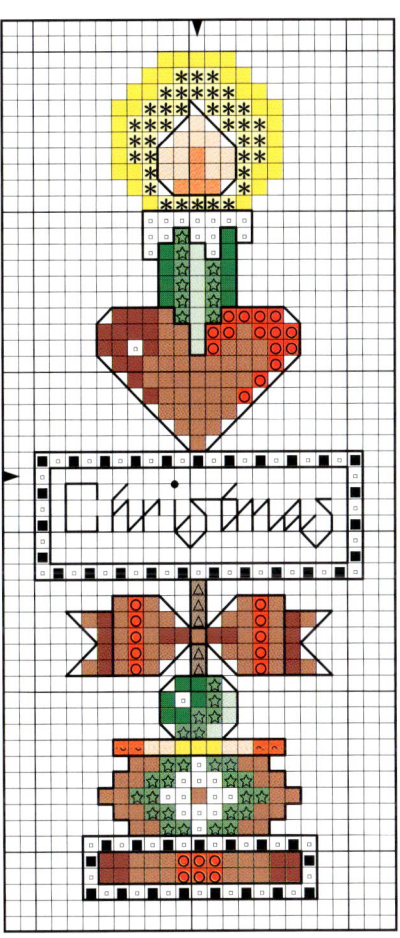

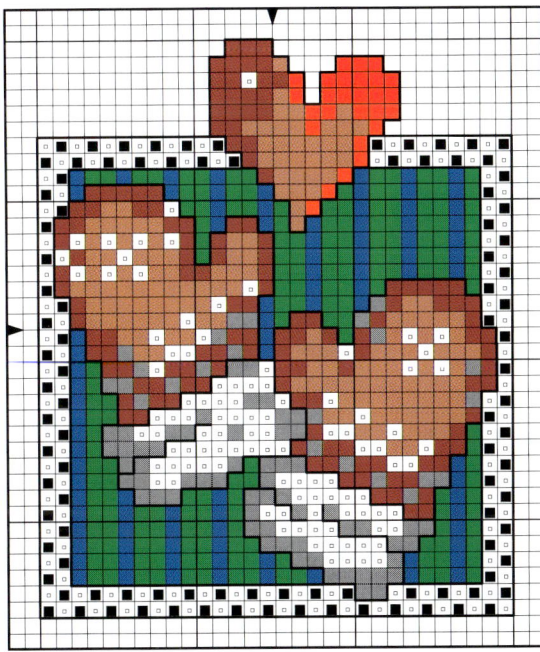

143

Design size: 30 wide x 36 high

Anchor	DMC
2	blanc
334	606
47	321
44	815
226	703
142	798
231	453
403	310

Backstitch: 403/310

201 Cross-Stitch Christmas Designs • 89

144

Design size: 36 wide x 19 high

Anchor	DMC	Backstitch (2 strands):
2	blanc	20/815—poles, bow, lettering
13	347	
9	352	146/322—remaining outlines
11	351	
314	741	
241	966	
128	775	
145	809	

145

Design size: 29 wide x 26 high

Anchor	DMC	
328	3341	**Eyelet** (star): 314/741
295	726	**Backstitch** (2 strands):
238	703	334/606—planet stripe
160	827	297/973—light rays
145	809	246/986—tree
146	322	147/797—remaining outlines

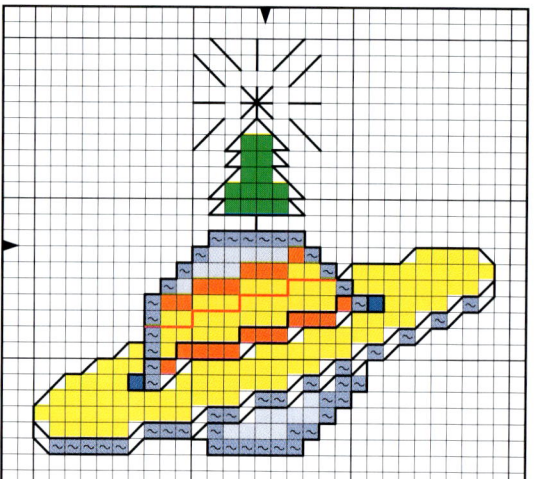

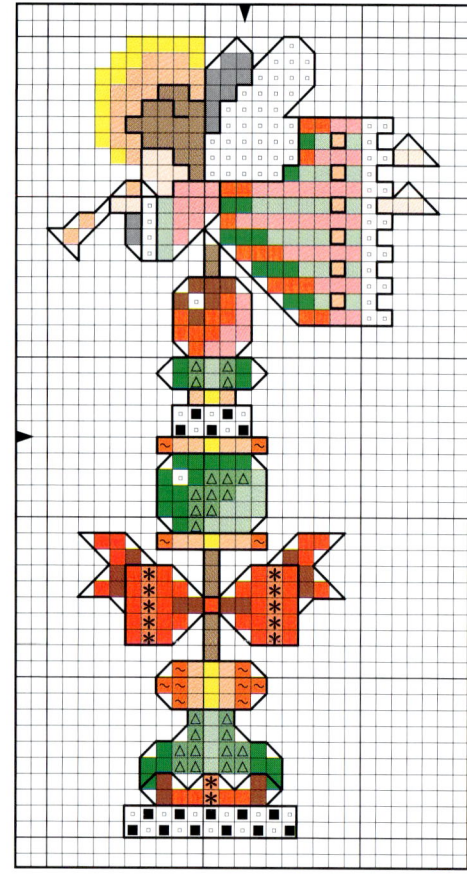

146

Design size: 25 wide x 50 high

Anchor	DMC
2	blanc
54	956
334	606
47	321
44	815
1012	754
314	741
326	720
302	743
226	703
229	910
923	699
1048	3776
231	453
403	310

Backstitch: 403/310

90 • *201 Cross-Stitch Christmas Designs*

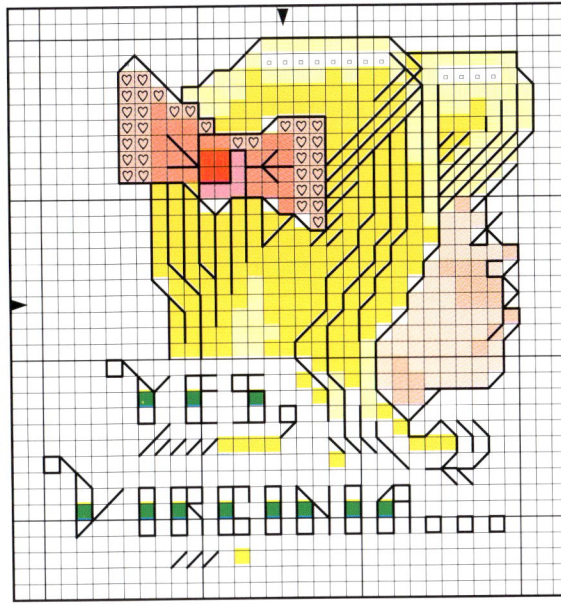

147

Design size: 31 wide x 33 high

Anchor	DMC
2	blanc
68	3687
13	347
778	3774
868	758
9	352
11	351
301	744
311	676
240	966

Backstitch (2 strands):
883/3064—face (except eye)
69/3687—bow
309/781—hair
210/562—lettering
145/809—eye

148

Design size: 22 wide x 41 high

Anchor	DMC
2	blanc
46	666
314	741
324	721
293	727
301	744
302	743
241	966
225	703
186	959
188	3812
128	775
129	809
177	792

Eyelets (tree, star): 316/970

Backstitch:
2/blanc (3 strands)—tree star outline
878/501—trees
176/793—frame, moon, stars

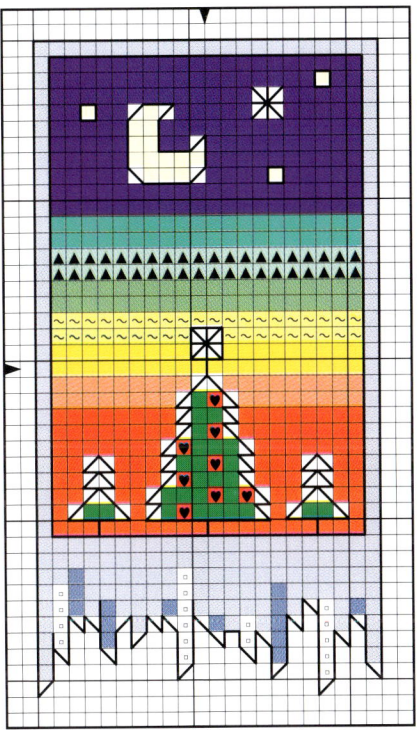

149

Design size: 29 wide x 30 high

Anchor	DMC
2	blanc
241	966
128	775
160	827

French Knots: 39/309
Eyelet (tree star): 302/743

Backstitch:
39/309—chimney
209/913—trees (except Christmas tree)
211/562—Christmas tree (except trunk)
161/813—snow, roof, icicles
978/322—frame
883/3064—remaining cabin, Christmas tree trunk
399/318—chimney smoke

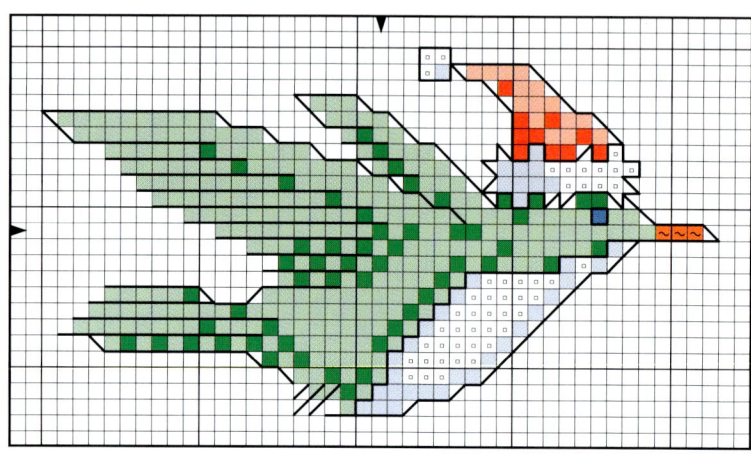

150

Design size: 43 wide x 23 high

Anchor	DMC
2	blanc
13	347
11	351
323	722
206	564
208	563
9159	3841
140	3755

Backstitch:
20/815—hat (except fur trims)
161/813—fur trims
162/825—bird

151

Design size: 38 wide x 21 high

Anchor	DMC
778	3774
42	326
9	352
11	351
337	3776
347	402
349	301

Backstitch:
43/814—bow
357/300—can

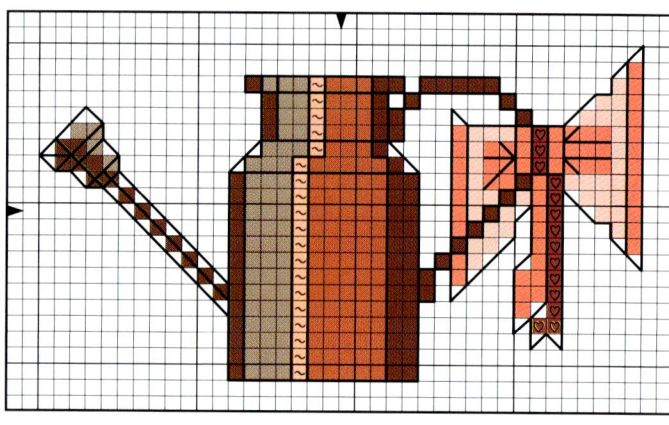

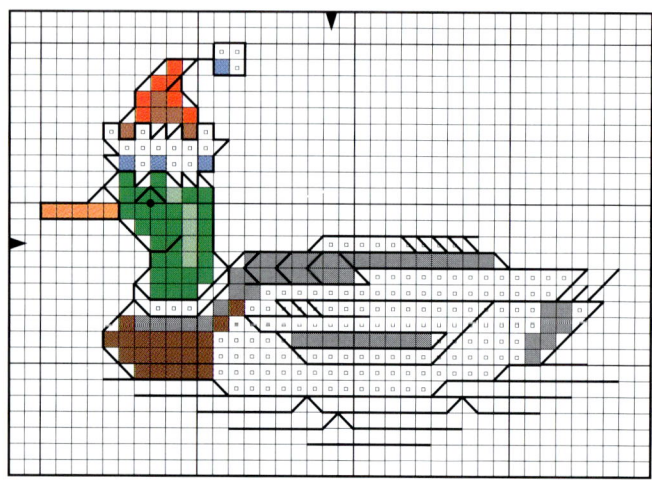

152

Design size: 37 wide x 25 high

Anchor	DMC
2	blanc
46	666
47	321
314	741
253	472
242	989
160	827
378	841
235	414

French Knot: 212/561
Backstitch:
1005/816—hat (except fur trim)
212/561—duck head (except beak), eyebrow
161/813—fur trim, water
371/434—remaining duck

153–164 Twelve Days of Christmas Baby Sampler

Design size: 178 wide x 218 high

Anchor	DMC	Anchor	DMC	Anchor	DMC	Anchor	DMC
2	blanc	303	742	185	964	347	436
386	3823	313	977	1032	3752	376	3774
361	738	314	741	128	775	349	301
24	963	329	3340	130	809	884	356
1022	760	300	745	160	827	379	840
1023	3712	301	744	129	800	936	632
334	606	1002	976	136	799	234	762
47	321	302	743	146	322	399	318
1006	304	311	676	142	798	235	414
86	3608	253	472	85	3609	400	317
778	754	225	703	1047	402	403	310
868	758	210	562	1048	3776		

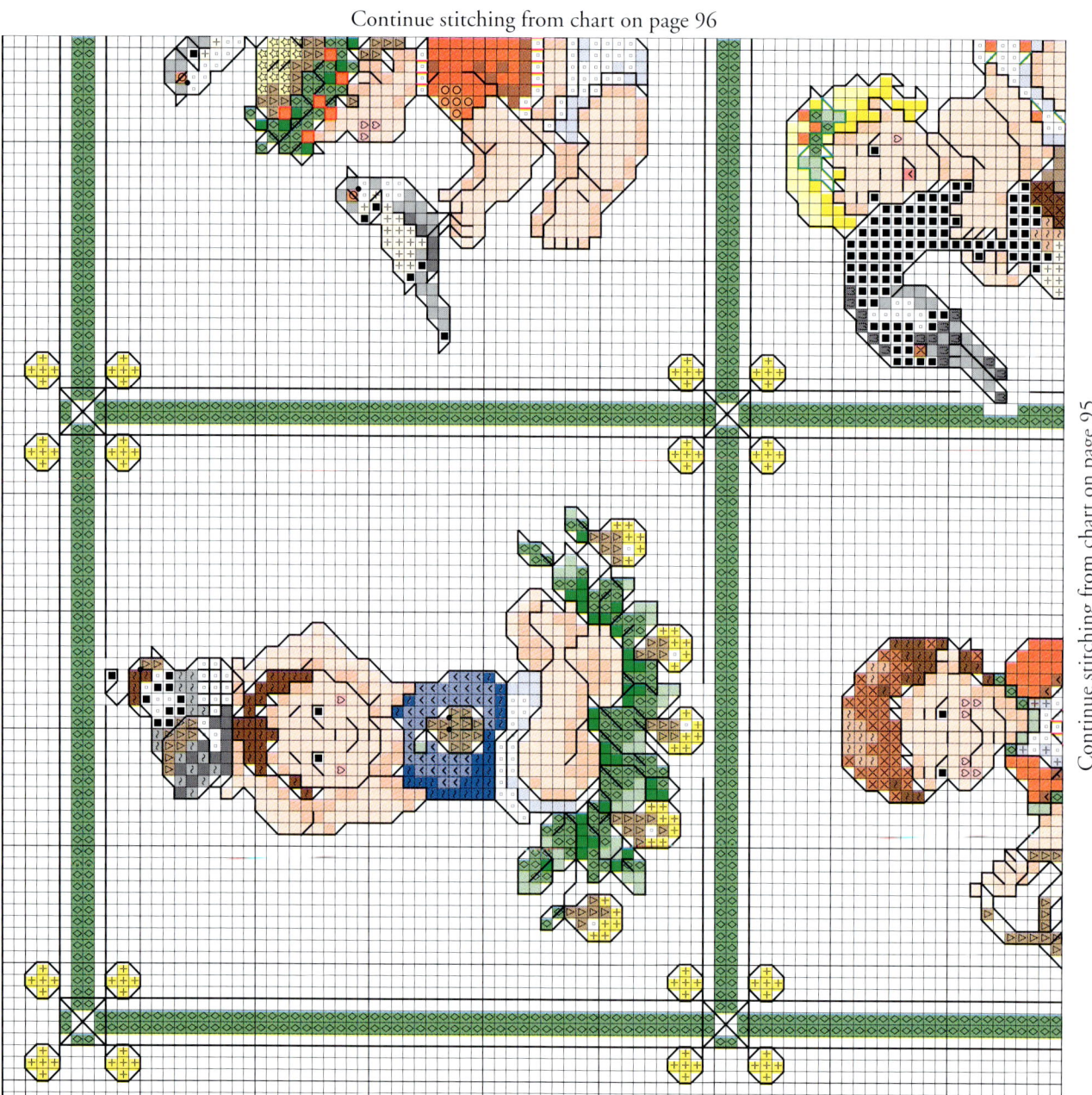

Continue stitching from chart on page 96

Continue stitching from chart on page 95

French Knots:
334/606—wheels
884/356—pear eyes
403/310—all bird eyes

Backstitch:
334/606—second day baby shirt stripes and berries; fourth day baby shirt stripes and overall patch outline; candy cane stripes, eighth day baby hat and apron stripes; nineth day baby streamers, panty stripe; balloon string, horn stripe; soldier's drum lines
1048/3776—straw
210/913—fourth day leaves and tree
211/562—sixth and 11th day leaves, inner tube, horn stripe
212/561—first and second day leaves
225/703—streamer, nineth day baby shirt design; 12th day string
131/798—water
146/322—streamer and wand star
936/632—seventh day baby skin and hair (including underwater foot), swan beak; 11th day baby hair
884/356—skin and hair (except eyes and seventh day baby skin), pears and pear stems, third day hen beaks and feet; bell, remaining horn, drumsticks
400/317—diapers (except 12th day diaper), first day baby shirt, second day baby remaining shirt and turtledoves, third day baby eyes, clothes, remaining hens; fourth day baby remaining clothes, red and blue birds; fifth day baby clothes, rings, bow, candy cane outlines and remaining outlines; sixth day goose (except eye), eggs; swan, seventh day baby clothes; eighth day baby clothes, calf (except eye), bow, bottle; nineth day baby remaining clothes, wand handle and shoes; 10th day remaining outlines; 11th day baby clothes and hat; 12th day diaper, soldier (except hat and shoes), remaining soldiers drum, platform and wheels.
403/310—partridge, baby eyes, remaining fourth day birds, 12th day baby soldier's hat and shoes, baby's shirt

Continue stitching from chart on page 97

Continue stitching from chart on page 94

201 Cross-Stitch Christmas Designs • 95

Continue stitching from chart on page 97

Continue stitching from chart on page 94

96 • 201 Cross-Stitch Christmas Designs

For color key see pages 94–95

Continue stitching from chart on page 96

Continue stitching from chart on page 95

201 Cross-Stitch Christmas Designs • 97

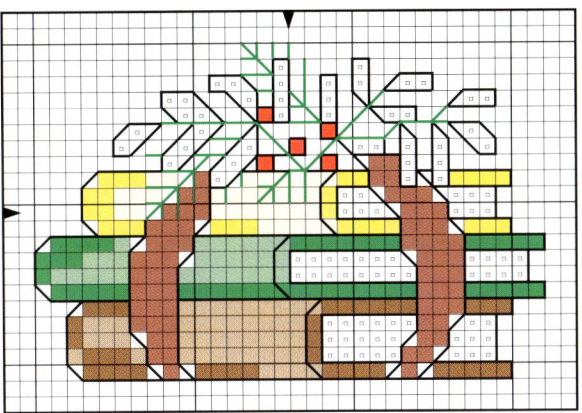

165

Design size: 32 wide x 21 high

Anchor	DMC
2	blanc
300	745
1025	347
896	3721
311	676
361	738
363	436
875	503
876	502

Backstitch:
877/501—branches, stems
400/317—remaining outlines

166

Design size: 34 wide x 28 high

Anchor	DMC
2	blanc
880	3774
13	347
6	754
10	351
128	775
160	827
882	758
884	356
400	317

Backstitch:
20/815—hat (except fur trim)
978/322—fur trim
351/400—dog (except eyes, nose, mouth)
403/310—eyes, nose, mouth

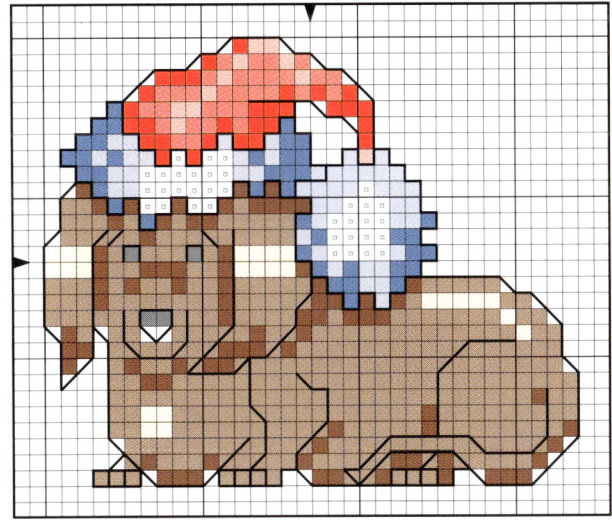

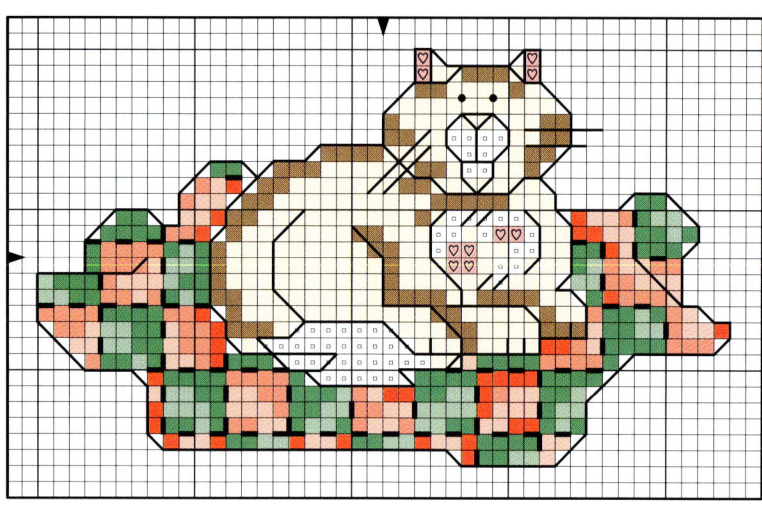

167

Design size:
44 wide x 26 high

	Anchor	DMC
	2	blanc
	361	738
	24	963
	13	347
	9	352
	11	351
	1047	402
	1043	369
	875	503

French Knots: 403/310

Backstitch:

877/501—(2 pt. line) blanket stitch lines
400/317—remaining outlines

168

Design size: 32 wide x 35 high

	Anchor	DMC
	2	blanc
	9	352
	11	351
	13	347
	778	3774
	868	758
	300	745
	891	676
	203	564
	205	912
	342	211
	109	209
	399	318

French Knots:
13/347—dress
400/317—eyes

Backstitch:
13/347—cuff stripes
400/317—remaining outlines

169

Design size: 82 wide x 52 high

Anchor	DMC
2	blanc
24	963
13	347
11	351
300	745
311	676
366	951
347	402
206	564
208	563

Anchor	DMC
210	562
1042	504
875	503
128	775
1008	3773
883	3064
234	762
399	318
403	310

French Knots:
146/322—stars
403/310—eyes, shoe and coat buttons

Eyelets (stars): 146/322

Backstitch:
146/322—snow
401/413—remaining outlines

170

Design size: 43 wide x 42 high

Anchor	DMC
2	blanc
334	606
47	321
44	815
314	741
300	745
302	743
226	703
229	910
1070	993
1074	992
108	210
110	208
397	3042
399	318

French Knots: 403/310

Backstitch:
44/815—flames, candles, ribbon
923/699—wreath
403/310—remaining outlines

171

Design size: 38 wide x 32 high

Anchor	DMC
2	blanc
9046	666
1005	816
1012	754
314	741
300	745
302	743
226	703
229	910
128	775
140	3755
1048	3776
351	400
403	310

Backstitch:
1005/816—berries, cuffs
142/798—wings, collar
923/699—leaves, remaining robe
351/400—skin, violin (except strings, bridge, tuning pegs)
403/310—remaining outlines

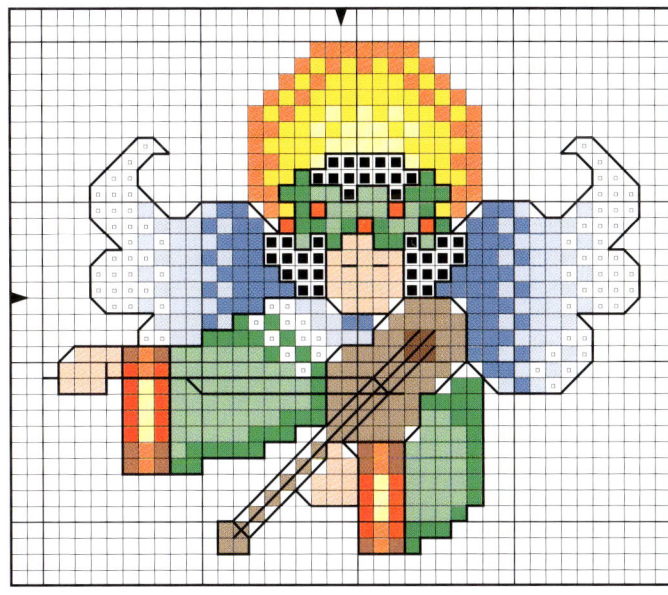

201 Cross-Stitch Christmas Designs • 103

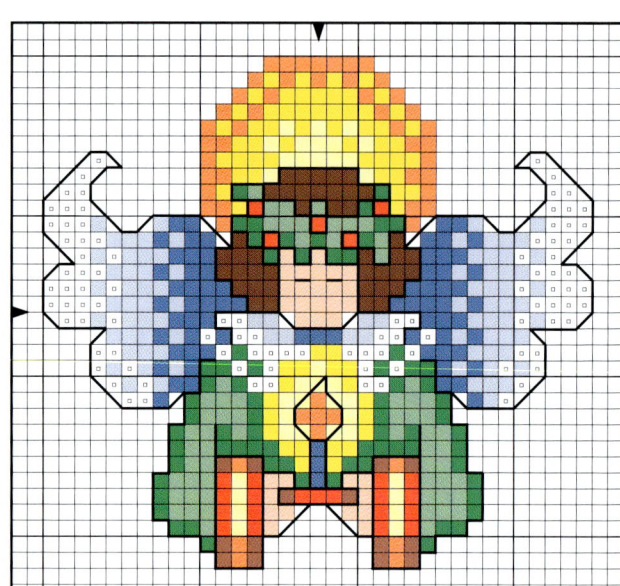

172

Design size: 35 wide x 32 high

Anchor	DMC
2	blanc
9046	666
1005	816
1012	754
314	741
300	745
302	743
226	703
229	910
128	775
140	3755
1004	920

Backstitch:
1005/816—berries, candle holder, cuffs
923/699—leaves, remaining robe
142/798—wings, candle, collar
351/400—hair, skin, flame

173

Design size: 35 wide x 29 high

Anchor	DMC
2	blanc
9046	666
1005	816
1012	754
314	741
326	720
300	745
302	743
226	703
229	910
128	775
140	3755

Backstitch:
1005/816—berries, cuffs
923/699—leaves, remaining robe
142/798—wings, collar
351/400—hair, skin, horn

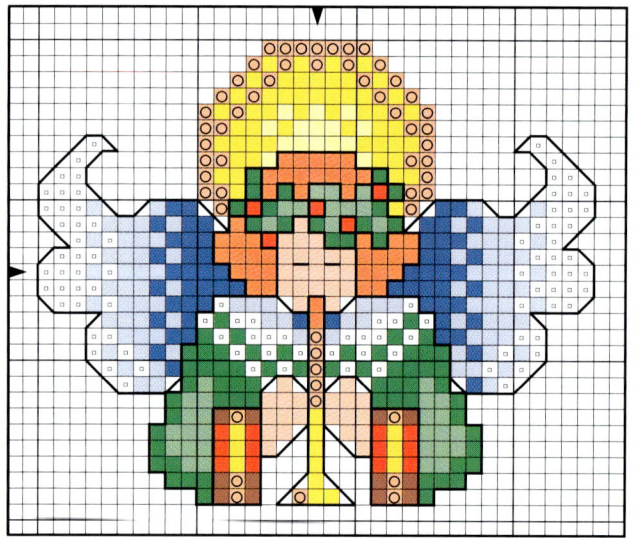

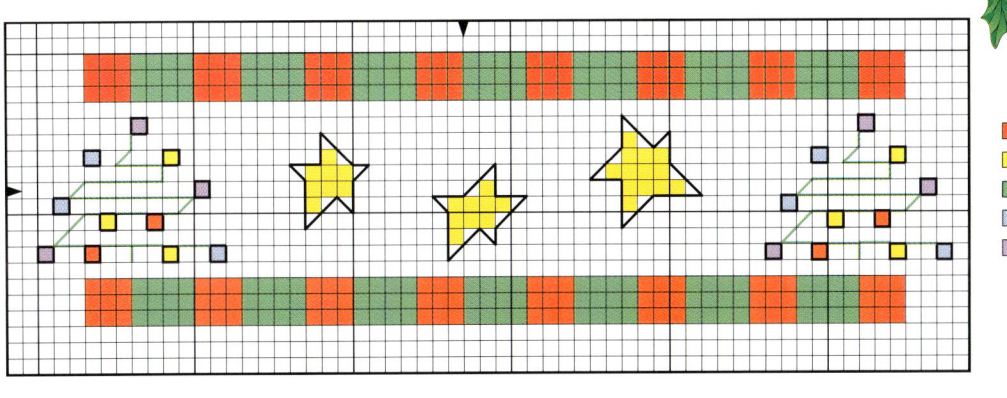

174

Design size: 54 wide x 17 high

	Anchor	DMC
■	46	666
■	311	676
■	241	966
■	1090	996
■	118	340

Backstitch:
210/562—trees
400/317—remaining outlines

201 Cross-Stitch Christmas Designs • 105

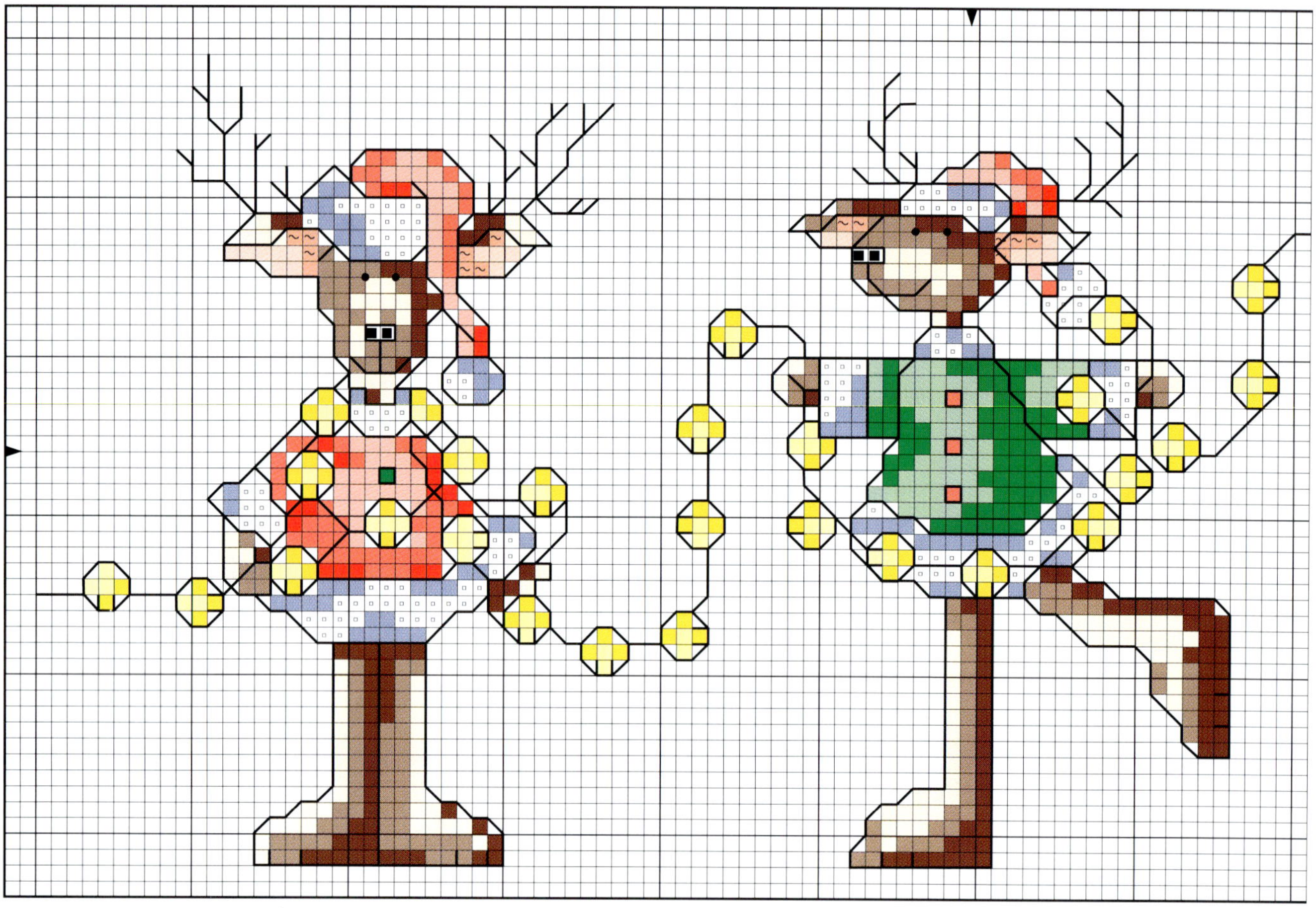

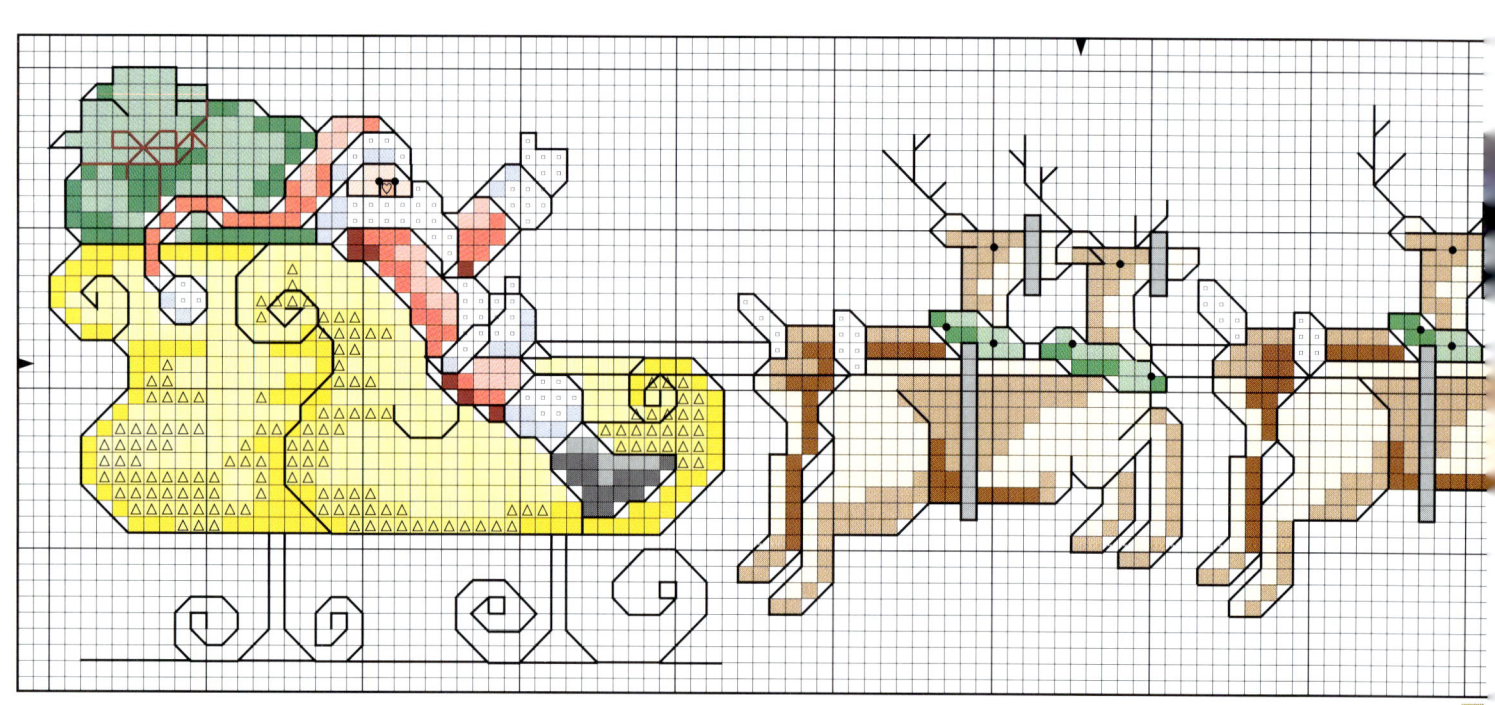

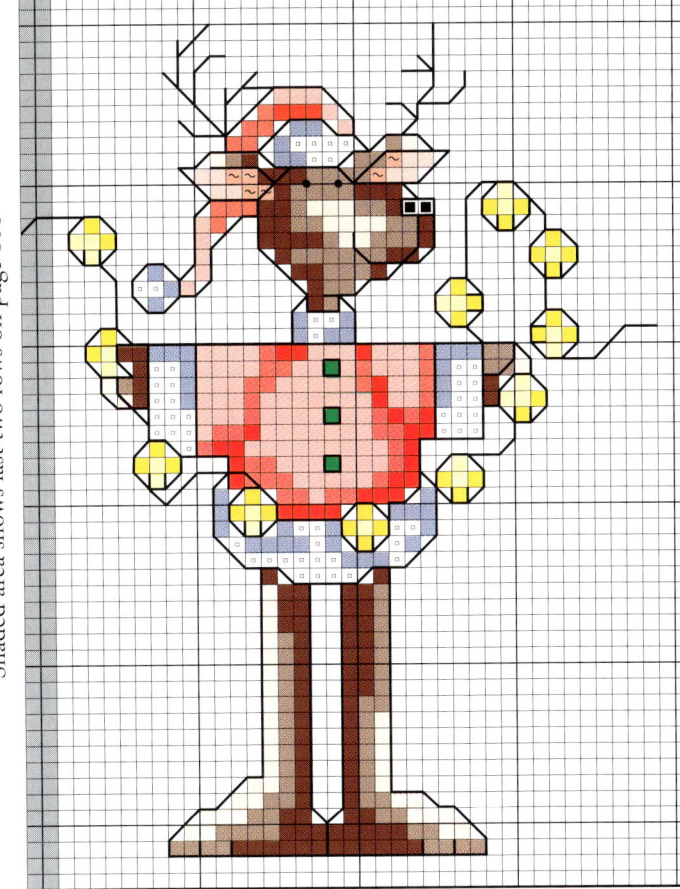

Shaded area shows last two rows on page 106

175

Design size: 119 wide x 52 high

	Anchor	DMC
·	2	blanc
☐	4146	950
■	47	321
	9	352
	11	351
	1012	754
~	6	761
	301	744
	302	743
	206	564
	208	563
	128	775
	337	3776
	379	840
■	403	310

French Knot: 403/310

Backstitch:
936/632—reindeer (except noses, mouths)
400/317—remaining outlines

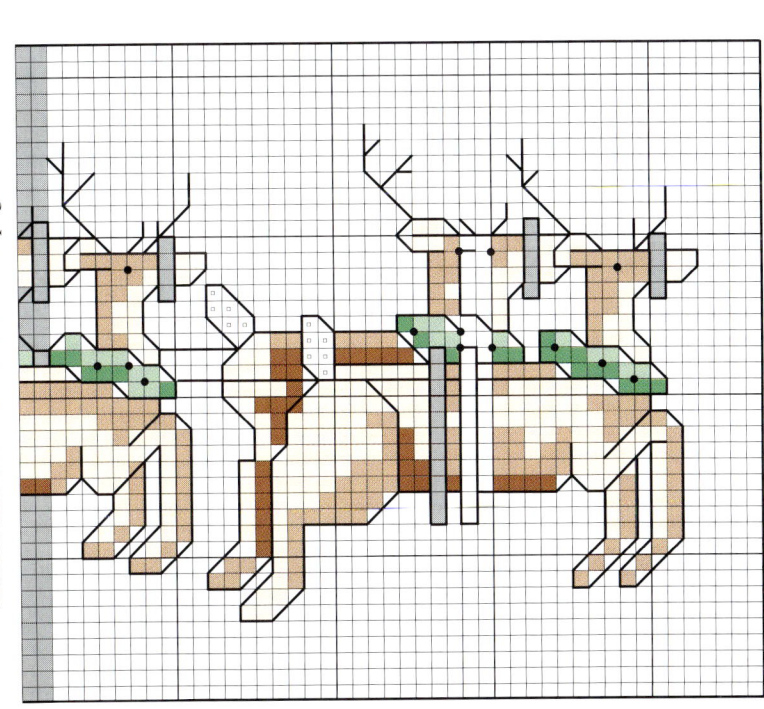

Shaded area shows last two rows on page 106

176

Design size: 131 wide x 37 high

	Anchor	DMC
·	2	blanc
☐	366	951
	47	321
	9	352
	11	351
	778	3774
♡	868	758
	300	745
△	311	676
	1002	977
	368	437
	369	435
	214	368
	216	502
	128	775
	398	415
■	235	414

French Knots:
47/321—berries
403/310—eyes

Backstitch:
47/321—tie on sack
400/317—remaining outlines

201 Cross-Stitch Christmas Designs • 107

177

Design size: 72 wide x 65 high

	Anchor	DMC
	2	blanc
■	46	666
~	47	321
✱	323	722
	305	743
	253	472
	225	703
	128	775
	160	827
△	161	813
	347	402
	400	317

French Knot: 403/310

Eyelets (castle stars): 305/743

Backstitch:

1005/816—pole, hat (except fur trim), bow, castle trim and stripes

349/301—door

332/946—beak

161/813—ice lines

978/322—fur trim, icicles, snow, letters, remaining castle

403/310—remaining penguin

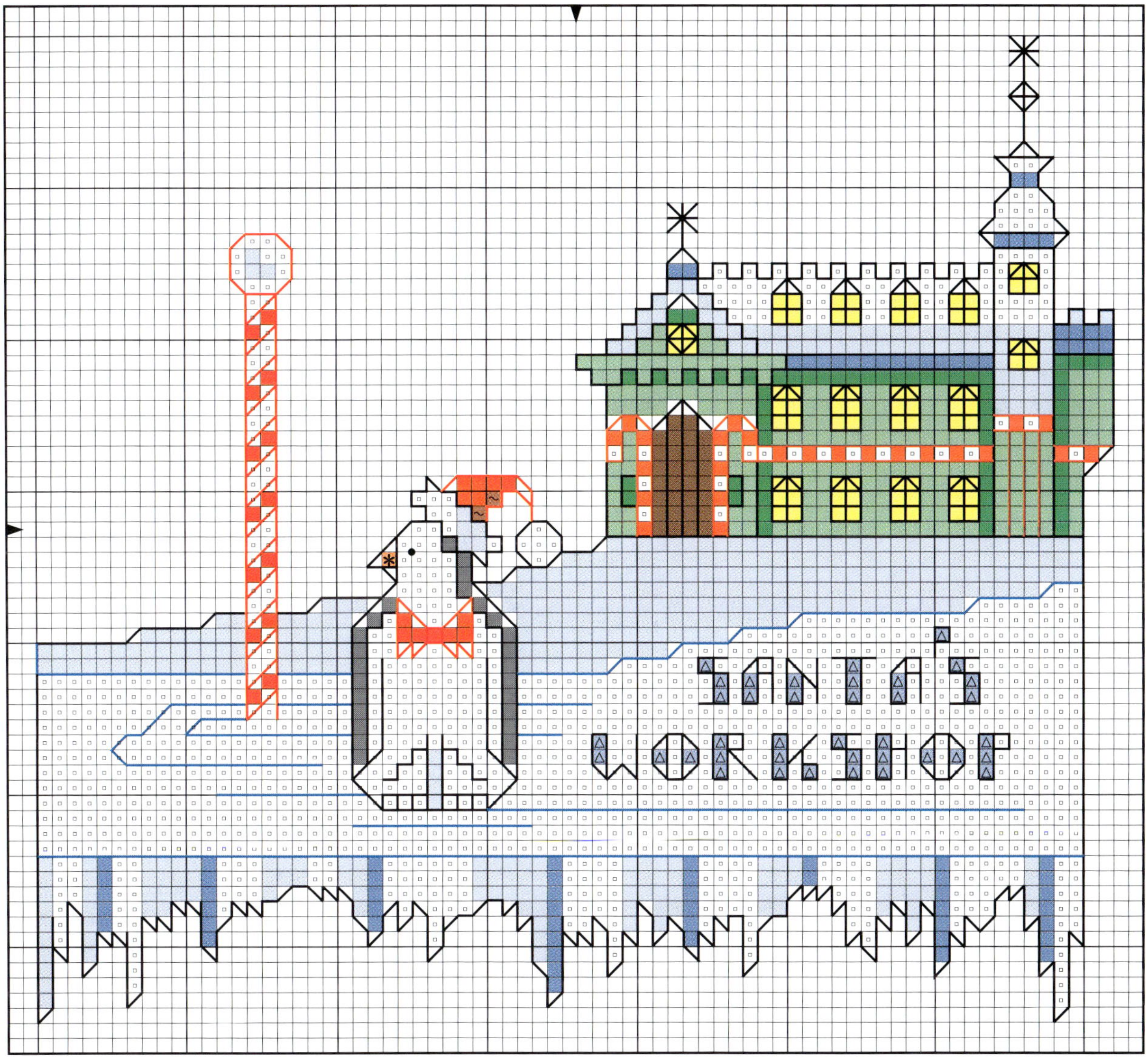

201 Cross-Stitch Christmas Designs • 109

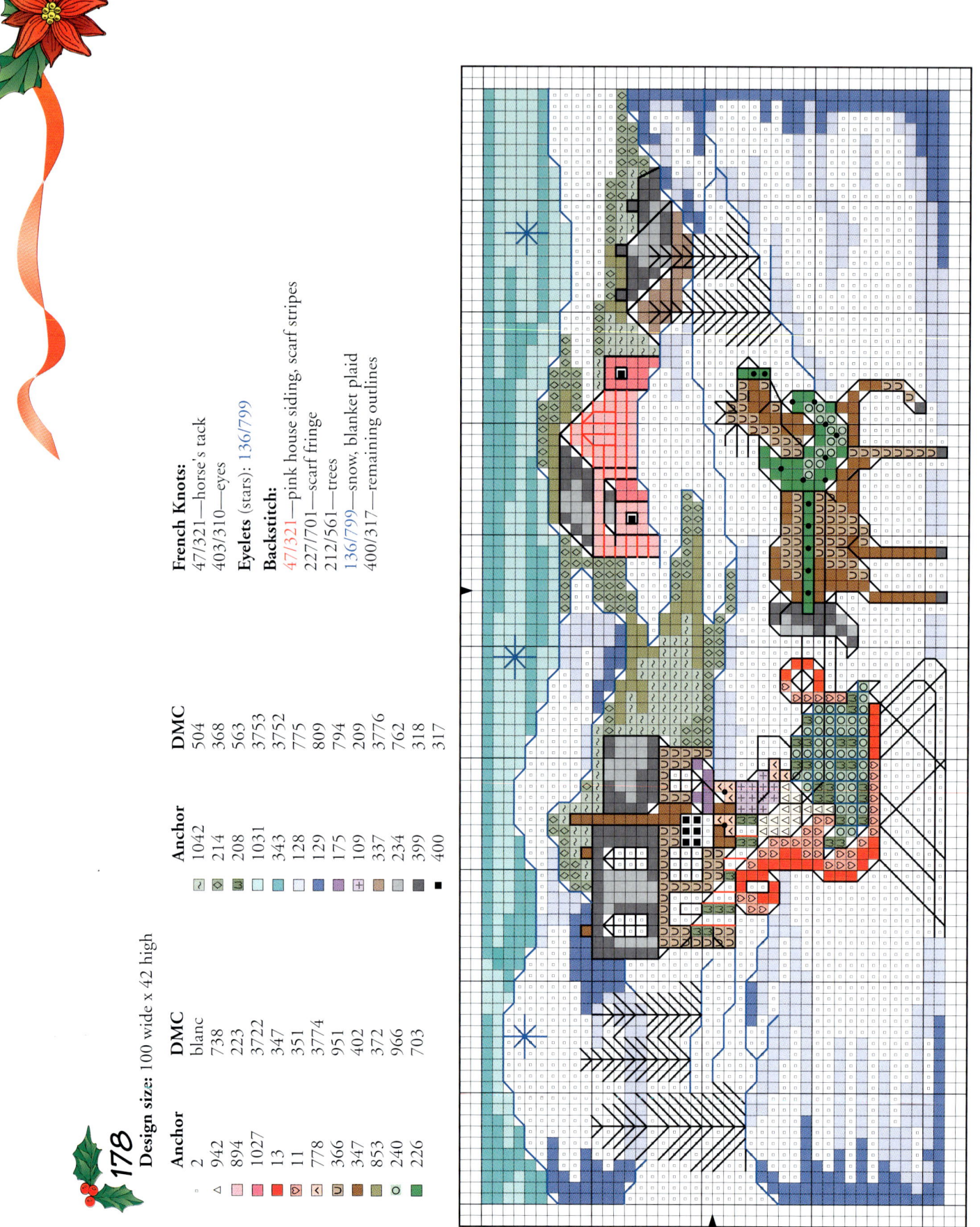

179

Design size: 57 wide x 73 high

Anchor	DMC
2	blanc
11	351
778	3774
301	744
226	703
1092	959
128	775
9159	3841
140	3755
1048	3776

Backstitch:
13/347—skater (except skates and hat fur trim)
208/563—top tree line
210/562—trees
161/813—snowflakes
162/825—borders, lettering, skates, hat fur trim, snow, ice, buildings (except doors, chimneys, windows, church cross)
87/3607—chimneys
1048/3776—windows, doors, hair
399/318—church cross, smoke

201 Cross-Stitch Christmas Designs • 111

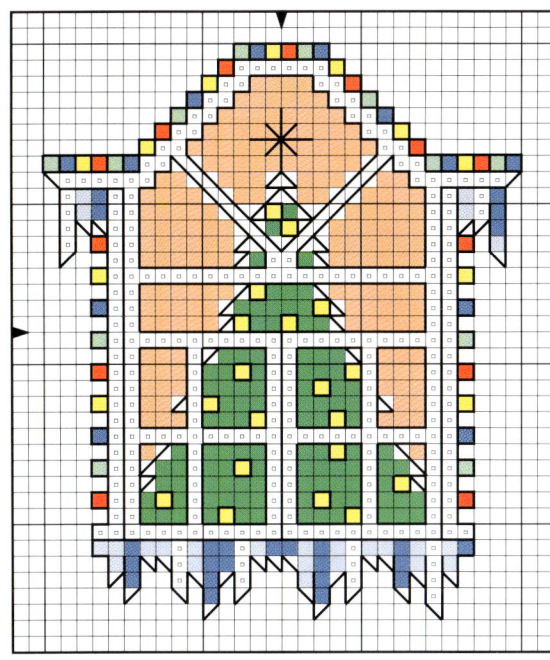

180

Design size: 30 wide x 36 high

Anchor	DMC
2	blanc
46	666
314	741
301	744
253	472
225	703
128	775
160	827

Eyelet (tree star): 305/743

Backstitch:
212/561—tree, tree lights
978/322—remaining outlines

181

Design size: 32 wide x 28 high

Anchor	DMC
2	blanc
11	351
302	744
242	989
128	775
110	208
369	435

Backstitch:
136/799—snow
936/632—remaining outlines

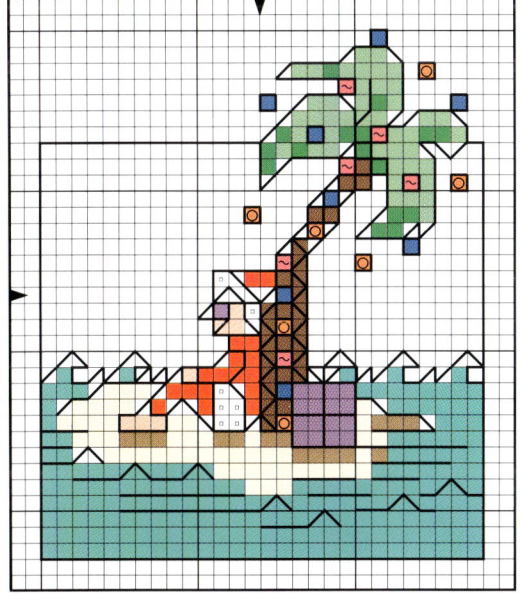

182

Design size: 28 wide x 33 high

Anchor	DMC
2	blanc
361	738
38	961
46	666
778	3774
303	742
363	436
240	966
243	703
185	964
160	827
96	3609
347	402

Backstitch:
1006/304—suit, hat
211/562—palm fronds
161/813—border, water
99/552—ornaments, sunglasses
349/301—skin and mouth, palm trunk

201 Cross-Stitch Christmas Designs • 113

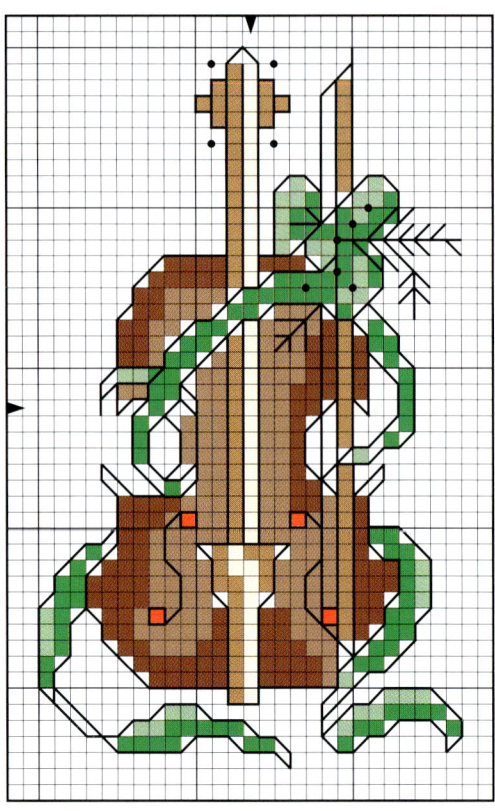

183

Design size: 27 wide x 45 high

Anchor	DMC
□ 885	739
■ 47	321
361	738
241	966
243	703
367	738
347	402

French Knots:
47/321—berries
401/413—tuning pegs

Backstitch:
210/562—pine needles
401/413—remaining outlines

184

Design size: 40 wide x 51 high

Anchor	DMC
2	blanc
778	3774
868	758
11	351
13	347
301	744
302	743
206	564
208	563
128	775
882	758
1007	3772
234	762
399	318

French Knots:
47/321—berries
403/310—eyes, shoes

Eyelets (stars): 136/799

Backstitch:
877/501—pine needles, leaf
136/799—snow
400/317—remaining outlines

185

Design size: 50 wide x 53 high

Anchor	DMC
386	3823
23	3713
31	3708
13	347
301	744
311	676
1002	977
203	564
1042	504
876	503
131	798

Backstitch:
878/501—leaves, tree
119/333—table
349/301—lettering
400/317—remaining outlines

201 Cross-Stitch Christmas Designs • 115

186–197 Twelve Days of Christmas Old Fashioned Sampler
Design size: 165 wide x 220 high

	Anchor	DMC		Anchor	DMC		Anchor	DMC
	2	blanc		1047	402		128	775
	300	745		1001	976		140	3755
	1024	3328		363	436		142	798
	50	3716		1048	3776		139	797
	54	956		255	907		108	210
	40	335		240	966		110	208
	1025	347		875	503		112	552
	29	309		257	905		369	435
	334	606		876	502		351	400
	47	321		246	986		371	434
	44	815		923	699		1004	920
	1005	816		683	890		899	3782
	1012	754		842	3013		903	640
	313	724		843	3053		905	3021
	314	741		848	927		231	453
	324	721		850	926		233	451
	326	720		1070	993		236	3799
	302	743		1074	992		403	310
	311	676		189	943			

French Knots: 403/310

Backstitch:
2/blanc—Partridge's eye, Calling Birds' eyes

Backstitch:
44/815—berries, Dove's pink flowers; Goose's red border; Lord's feather and sash; Maid's red dress trim and bow

1005/816—Ring's rose; Swan's pink flowers and buds; Lady's pink and red dress edges, flowers in hair and at waist and large rose

314/741 (2 strands)—Lady's border

326/720—Swan's yellow and orange flowers and buds and border; Lady's fan and gold dress border

1048/3776—nest, Piper's skin

246/986—leaves (except Ring's leaves), trees, stems (except Partridge's stems), green dress edges, Lady's shoes; Lord's hat and collar trim

683/890—Ring's leaves and large gem

923/699—Piper's banner on horn

843/3053—grass

139/797—Dove's blue and purple flowers; Piper's hat, clothes and stockings; Drummer's blue hat edges and blue coat edges

140/3755—snowdrifts

146/322—Ring's blue flowers

189/943—Ring's bow

112/552—Swan's purple flowers and buds

351/400—pears (except bottom "v"), rings, houses, hair (except Piper and Drummer), cows

360/898—basket; Piper's hair, horn and shoes

371/434—Drummer's hair, pants, shoes

1004/920—skin (except Piper); Lord's bubbles, cuffs and shirt hem; Drummer's hat band, drum strap, coat cuffs and hem and dog

401/413—Doves, remaining Lady's dress

403/310—remaining outlines

Continue stitching from chart on page 119

Continue stitching from chart on page 120

118 • *201 Cross-Stitch Christmas Designs*

For color key see page 117

Continue stitching from chart on page 118

Continue stitching from chart on page 121

Continue stitching from chart on page 118

Continue stitching from chart on page 121

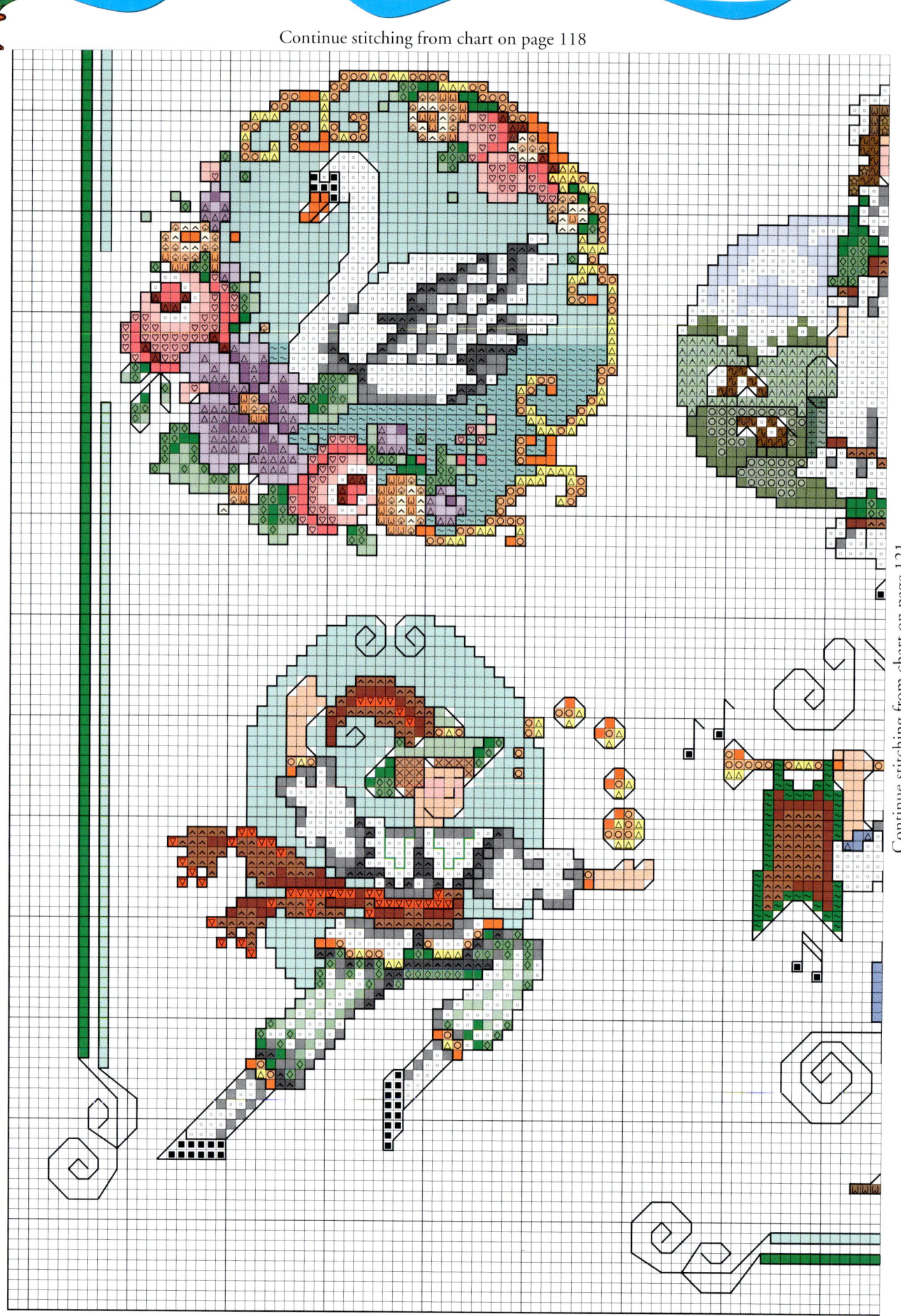

For color key see page 117

Continue stitching from chart on page 119

Continue stitching from chart on page 120

201 Cross-Stitch Christmas Designs • 121

198

Design size: 41 wide x 17 high

Anchor	DMC
2	blanc
386	437
778	3774
868	758
301	744
311	676
1047	402

French Knots: 235/414

Backstitch: 235/414

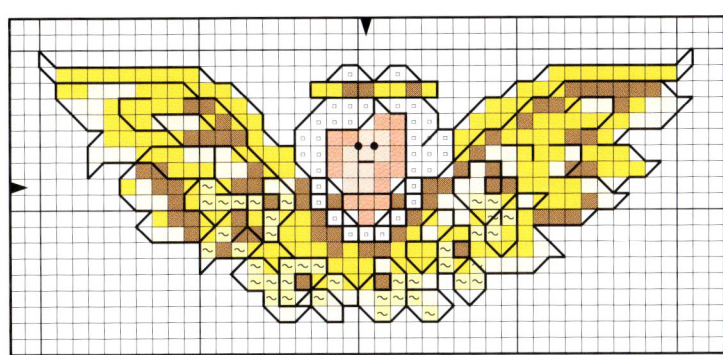

199

Design size: 36 wide x 20 high

Anchor	DMC
2	blanc
868	758
328	3341
301	744
1002	977
260	3364
265	3347

Backstitch:
20/815—rose outlines
329/3340—remaining roses
333/608—strings
878/501—leaves
936/632—buds, branches
235/414—fan

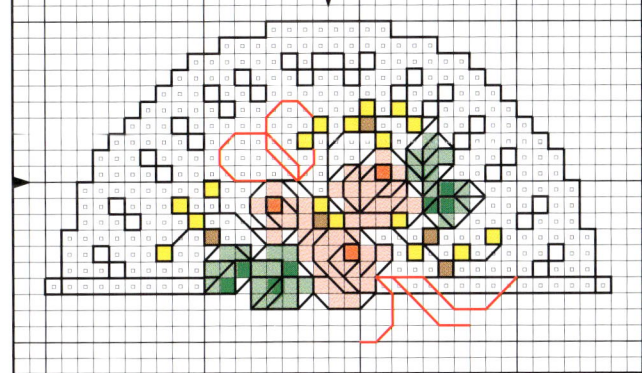

201 Cross-Stitch Christmas Designs • 123

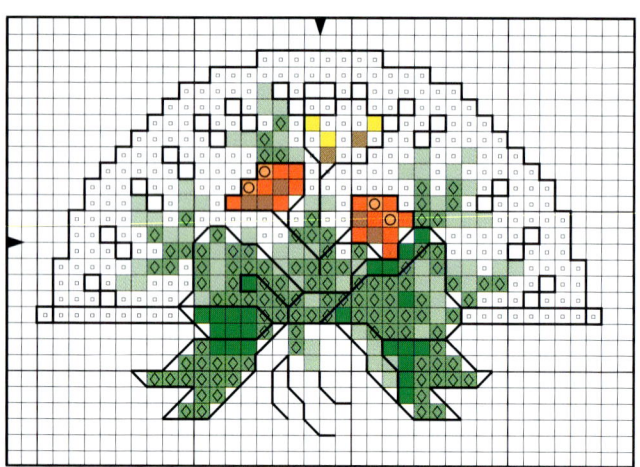

200

Design size: 36 wide x 24 high

Anchor	DMC
2	blanc
46	666
47	321
323	722
301	744
1002	977
264	3348
266	3347
210	562

Backstitch:
20/815—red flowers
1049/301—white flower
210/562—stems, ribbons
235/414—fan

201

Design size: 36 wide x 22 high

Anchor	DMC
2	blanc
46	666
778	3774
882	758
367	738
1045	436
240	966
210	562
234	762

French Knot: 235/414

Backstitch:
1005/816—buds
884/356—skin
370/434—hair
211/561—leaves, stems
235/414—fan, wings

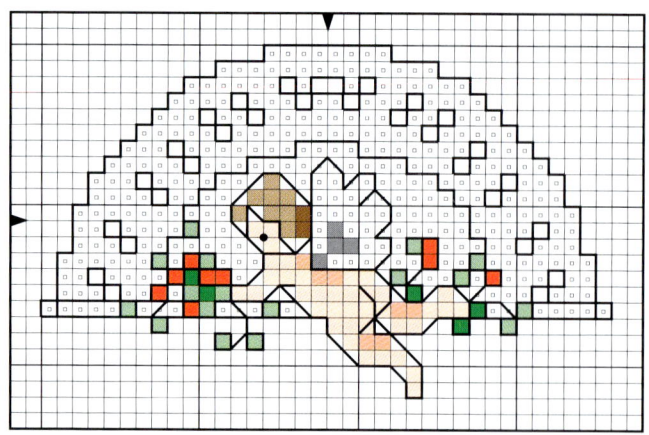

Finishing Information

FINISHING NEEDLEWORK

Wash stitched fabric in cool water with a gentle soap. Rinse well. Roll in a towel and squeeze out excess moisture. Place face down on a dry towel and iron carefully. Frame or finish as desired.

To make perforated plastic or paper ornaments or package ties, stitch the design; then cut excess at least one space beyond all stitches. Glue one or two larger pieces of felt or paper to the wrong side with a hanging loop sandwiched in between; then trim edges as desired.

For gift bags, trim excess fabric from design. Center and glue onto purchased gift bag. Glue ribbon to edge of design, overlapping one or two rows of stitches.

To make wreath frames, cut a piece of backing, such as foam board, the same size as wreath. Attach design to right side of backing by folding excess fabric over edges of backing and pinning or gluing fabric to backing. Center design under wreath and glue back of wreath to front of design. Draw a ribbon through bells and weave ribbon ends through wreath. Tie a knot to secure ribbon on back of wreath. Cut a length of ribbon to make a bow and glue to front of wreath.

For bell pulls, use purchased hangers. Sew the side edges of the fabric to make a sleeve; then fold top and bottom edges over hangers and secure in place. Trim as desired. For an alternate bell pull, sew side edges of the fabric and then fold bottom edges together to make a point. Then fold top and bottom edges over a hanger and secure in place. Trim as desired.

For hanging pieces, sew side and bottom edges of fabric to make a pocket; then fold top edge over a dowel, cut slightly longer than piece. Cut a length of ribbon twice the length of the dowel. Tie an end of ribbon to each end of the dowel, making a bow on each side. Hang piece from purchased hanger.

To make a pillow, sew a fabric border of equal width around edges of stitched piece. Cut another piece of fabric the same size as the stitched piece and borders. With right sides together, sew along edges of fabric, leaving a small opening to turn right side out. Turn right side out and stuff with soft batting or fiber-fill. Sew opening closed.

Index of Charts
by Subject Matter

Airplane 23
Angel........................61, 69, 90, 103, 104, 123, 124
Baby......................79, 94, 95, 96, 97
Baseball 47
Bear..75
Bells 29, 83
Bicycle.......................................39, 69
Bird..92
Birdhouse 56, 72, 83
Bone 15
Books...99
Butterfly 52
Candle 14, 44, 63
Candy 64
Car..72
Carolers...30
Cat...100, 103
Children....................19, 80, 91, 115
Clock 67
Computer 67
Cooking...........................39, 55, 85
Decorations.............36, 56, 57, 89, 90
Dog...79, 99
Elf 70
Fan...123, 124
Fireplace....................................43, 67
Fishing...40
Football...47
Fruit...60
Gate...90
Gingerbread Man 27
Golf 41, 46
Heart..89
Horse...76

Houses 17, 29, 32, 91
Landscape 32, 33, 50, 91, 110, 111
Lettering 16, 20, 25, 50, 53, 55, 57, 59, 86, 115
Mittens 89
Mouse 101
North Pole 26, 109
Nutcracker 13
Ornament 16, 70, 73, 86
Outer Space 17, 22, 25, 90
Penguin................................15, 26
Pig...52
Plant 17, 35, 60, 61, 63, 80, 82
Presents 60, 70, 100, 103
Rabbit..75
Reindeer...............77, 83, 106, 107
Samplers.....................6, 7, 8, 9, 10, 11, 38, 39, 40, 41, 94, 95, 96, 97, 118, 119, 120, 121
Santa 6, 7, 8, 9, 10, 11, 22, 23, 25, 38, 39, 40, 41, 64, 66, 106
Shoes......................................22, 32, 33
Snowflake......................................82
Snowman 27, 57, 80
Stars 36, 87, 105
Stockings..........................43, 67, 73
Tennis 39, 41, 46
Toys 44, 49, 63, 66, 69, 70, 72, 75, 76, 77, 100
Train 69, 87
Tree 56, 63, 87, 89, 113
Violin..114
Watering Can...............................92
Water Sports............38, 39, 40, 41, 49
Wreath 53

General Directions

FABRICS, NEEDLES, AND THREADS

These designs were cross-stitched on 14-count fabric, vinyl, or perforated plastic or paper. On 14-count fabrics, two strands of floss are usually used. On 14-count vinyl or perforated surfaces, three strands are recommended because the area over which each stitch is made is relatively small.

Use a blunt-tipped tapestry needle, size 24 or 26, for most stitching. The higher the number, the smaller the needle. The most commonly used thread for counted cross-stitch is six-strand cotton embroidery floss. Divide it into individual strands; then put the required number back together before threading the needle.

Our photographed models were stitched with Anchor embroidery floss and the DMC floss numbers are also listed. The companies have different color ranges, so these are only suggested color substitutions. A "blended" color is noted in the color key as two numbers separated by a slash; use one strand of each floss color.

WORKING FROM CHARTED DESIGNS

Each square on a chart corresponds to a space for a cross-stitch on the stitching surface. The color in a square shows the floss color to be used for the stitch. The chart colors are not necessarily close matches for the actual floss colors. They have been charted to provide contrast for ease in reading the charts. Often a symbol has been added to the color square to provide even more contrast.

The chart is accompanied by a color key which lists the numbers of the floss colors to be used. The design stitch width and height are given; centers are shown by arrows.

Straight lines over or between squares indicate backstitches or straight stitches. Eyelets are shown by their shapes, and French knots by dots. Occasionally color is used for lines and dots to help differentiate the colors to be used. For other charts, a thicker line is used for further clarification.

GETTING STARTED

To begin in an unstitched area, bring threaded needle to front of fabric. Hold an inch of the end against the back; then anchor it with your first few stitches. To end threads and begin new ones next to existing stitches, weave through the backs of several stitches.

THE STITCHES

Cross-stitch

The cross-stitch is formed in two motions. Follow the numbering in **Fig 1** and bring needle up at 1, down at 2, up at 3, down at 4, to complete the stitch. Work horizontal rows of stitches, **Fig 2,** wherever possible. Bring thread up at 1, work half of each stitch across the row, then complete the stitches on your return.

Fig 1

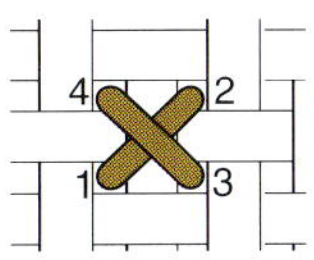

Fig 2

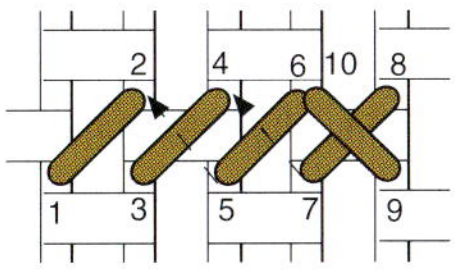

Backstitch

Backstitches are worked after cross-stitches have been completed. They may slope in any direction and are occasionally worked over more than one square of fabric. **Fig 3** shows the progression of several stitches; bring thread up at odd numbers and down at even numbers.

Frequently you must choose where to end one backstitch color and begin the next color. Choose the object that should appear closest to you. Backstitch around that shape with the appropriate color; then backstitch the areas behind it with adjacent color(s). Occasionally a color key will have two backstitch symbols (a thick line and a thin one), or colored lines to help you differentiate colors.

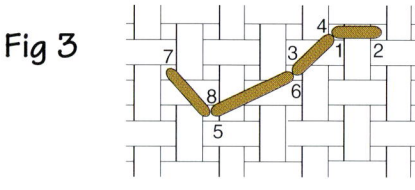

Fig 3

Eyelet

This is a technique that produces a starburst effect. Bring thread up at any point along the outside of the charted shape, **Fig 4,** and stitch down into the center. Continue to work around the shape as shown on the chart, always entering at center of eyelet. Occasionally the color key will use colored lines to help differentiate the floss colors.

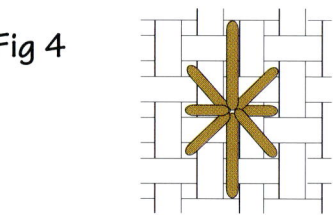

Fig 4

French Knot

Bring thread up where indicated on chart. Wrap floss once around needle, **Fig 5,** and reinsert needle at 2, close to 1, but at least one fabric thread away from it. Hold wrapping thread tightly and pull needle through, letting thread go just as knot is formed. For a larger knot, use more strands of floss, but wrap only once. Occasionally the color key will use colored dots to help differentiate the floss colors to be used.

Fig 5

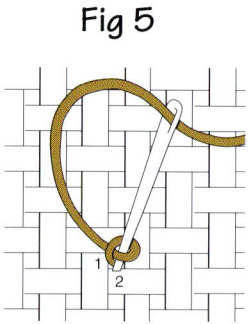

Straight Stitch

A straight stitch, **Fig 6,** is made like a long backstitch. Come up at one end of the stitch and down at the other. Follow the chart for exact placement. Occasionally the color key will use colored lines to help differentiate the floss colors.

Fig 6

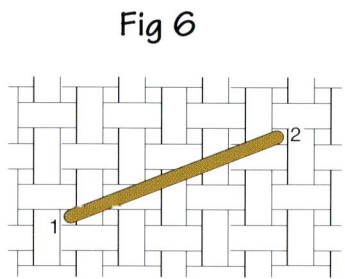

126 • 201 Cross-Stitch Christmas Designs